NORTHERN IRELAND
A WALKING
GUIDE

NORTHERN IRELAND
A WALKING
GUIDE

HELEN FAIRBAIRN

The Collins Press

Published in 2006 by
The Collins Press
West Link Park
Doughcloyne
Wilton
Cork

British Library Cataloguing in Publication Data
Fairbairn, Helen
          Northern Ireland: a walking guide
          1. Walking - Northern Ireland -
          Guidebooks
          2. Hiking - Northern Ireland - Guidebooks
          3. Northern Ireland - Guidebooks
          I. Title
          914.1'6'04824
          ISBN-10: 1905172214
          ISBN-13: 978-1905172214

          Typesetting: The Collins Press

          Font: RotisSansSerif, 12 point

          Printed in Malta

TABLE OF CONTENTS

Acknowledgements

Many thanks to those who accompanied me on research trips for this guide: Diane, Eoghan, John and Mac the dog. Most of all thanks to Gareth for extended company, support and mapwork.

Edited versions of many of these routes have previously appeared in *Walking World Ireland*.

Disclaimer

We have made every effort to ensure the information in this book is accurate. However, recognised pathways do change and walking, by its very nature, can be a hazardous activity. No responsibility is accepted by the author or publisher for any loss, injury or inconvenience sustained by anyone using this book.

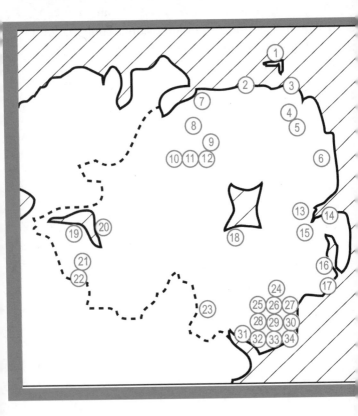

Route No	Walk Name	Location	Category
1	Rathlin Island	Antrim	Coastal Walk
2	Antrim Cliff Path	Antrim	Coastal Walk
3	Fair head & Murlough Bay	Antrim	Coastal Walk
4	Trostan & the Moyle Way	Antrim	Hill Walk
5	Glenariff Forest Park	Antrim	Woodland/ Hill Walk
6	Shane's Hill to Glenarm	Antrim	Hill Walk
7	Binevenagh Cliffs	Derry	Hill Walk
8	Roe Valley Country Park	Derry	Waterside Walk
9	Banagher Glen & Forest	Derry	Woodland Walk
10	The Western Sperrins	Tyrone	Hill Walk
11	Sawel & Dart Mountains	Derry/Tyrone	Hill Walk
12	The Eastern Sperrins	Derry/Tyrone	Hill Walk
13	Cave Hill	Belfast	Hill Walk
14	North Down Coastal Path	Down	Coastal Walk
15	Lagan Towpath	Antrim/Down	Waterside Walk
16	Castle Ward	Down	Waterside/ Woodland Walk
17	Ballyhornan Coastal Path	Down	Coastal Walk

Route No	Walk Name	Location	Category
18	Peatlands Park	Armagh	Woodland Walk
19	Cliffs of Magho	Fermanagh	Hill/ Woodland Walk
20	Castle Archdale	Fermanagh	Waterside/ Woodland Walk
21	Marble Arch & Florence Court	Fermanagh	Hill/ Woodland Walk
22	Cuilcagh Mountain	Fermanagh	Hill Walk
23	Slieve Gullion	Armagh	Hill/ Woodland Walk
24	Tollymore Forest Park	Down	Woodland Walk
25	Slieve Meelmore & Slieve Meelbeg	Down	Hill Walk
26	Slieve Commedagh	Down	Hill Walk
27	Slieve Donard	Down	Hill Walk
28	Slieve Bearnagh & the Silent Valley	Down	Hill Walk
29	The Brandy Pad	Down	Hill Walk
30	Annalong Valley	Down	Hill Walk
31	Rostrevor Forest	Down	Hill Walk
32	Rocky River Circuit	Down	Hill Walk
33	Eagle Mountain	Down	Hill Walk
34	The Binnians	Down	Hill Walk

Grade	Distance	Ascent	Time	Page
1	9km (5^1/$_2$ miles)	40m (130ft)	2-3 hrs	121
2	5km (3 miles)	300m (985ft)	2-2^1/$_2$ hrs	127
1	10km (6 miles)	60m (200ft)	2^1/$_2$-3^1/$_2$ hrs	133
2	11km (7 miles)	280m (920ft)	3-4 hrs	139
4	16km (10 miles)	540m (1770ft)	6-7 hrs	145
3	12.5km (8 miles)	500m (1640ft)	4-5 hrs	151
2	10km (6 miles)	370m (1210ft)	3-4 hrs	157
4	11km (7 miles)	685m (2250ft)	4-5 hrs	163
4	10km (6 miles)	780m (2560ft)	4-5 hrs	169
4	9km (5^1/$_2$ miles)	850m (2800ft)	4-5 hrs	175
4	11km (7 miles)	850m (2800ft)	5-6 hrs	181
3	11km (7 miles)	420m (1380ft)	4-5 hrs	187
5	17.5km (11 miles)	1080m (3450ft)	7-8 hrs	193
2	3.5km (2 miles)	265m (870ft)	1^1/$_2$-2 hrs	199
4	12km (7^1/$_2$ miles)	875m (2870ft)	5-6 hrs	205
3	8km (5 miles)	490m (1610ft)	3-4 hrs	211
4	13km (8 miles)	625m (1900ft)	4^1/$_2$ -5^1/$_2$ hrs	217

WALKING IN NORTHERN IRELAND: AN INTRODUCTION

Northern Ireland, situated in the northeastern corner of Ireland, encompasses six of the nine counties of Ulster. Measuring just 130km by 150km, the region packs an impressive variety of scenery into a relatively compact area.

The flat centre drains to Lough Neagh, the largest lake in Ireland at 383km^2. Around the shores of the lough lie the region's heartland, a low-lying landscape largely taken up by agricultural farm land.

Beyond this the ground rises to a series of rolling hills, with the most significant mountain ranges scattered around the periphery of the region. 'Mountain' is of course a relative term – Northern Ireland's highest peaks wouldn't even register as hills in some countries. Yet many of the upland walks start at sea level and it isn't uncommon for a route to include 800m or more of vertical ascent: a respectable day's toil no matter where you are in the world.

In terms of topography the region's crowning glory is the Mourne Mountains, which include Slieve Donard, the highest summit in Ulster at 850m. Rising directly from the sea in the southeast of the region, no walker should spend long in Northern Ireland without a visit to the Mournes. Other ranges of note include the Sperrin Mountains in the central west, the Antrim Hills in the north and the Fermanagh uplands in the southwest.

First-time visitors to Northern Ireland are often surprised by the lack of trees covering the hills. Most open ground is indeed bereft of vegetation more than ankle high and a long history of forest clearance means native woods are a precious commodity. The occasional pocket of ancient woodland does exist but managed pine plantations are now much more common.

The Atlantic Ocean and Irish Sea define the region's border to the north and east, providing a lengthy coastline that is another of the region's most treasured habitats. The World Heritage Site of the Giant's Causeway is the most famous feature of the north coast, though the neighbouring cliffs and beaches are equally dramatic. Further south, the shoreline of County Down is less publicised but also harbours some beautiful coastal scenery.

Northern Ireland has much to explore, and this guide details a variety of routes in all the best areas. Whether you prefer mountain treks, woodland walks or coastal paths, there's no better way to discover the real diversity of the region than on foot.

WALKING PRACTICALITIES

Northern Ireland's political troubles have deterred many people from visiting the region over the last 40 years. Locals have always enjoyed the countryside however, and the result is a region with some great walking routes but relatively little exploitation of their potential. Many of the remote routes come with a virtual guarantee of solitude – a novel experience for anyone used to crowded trails overseas.

Around half the routes in this book explore managed reserves or follow waymarked ways. These routes usually follow formal footpaths and are signposted to some degree. In the hills it is a different story; here, self reliance is the name of the game. Informal paths may have formed over popular peaks but they should not be relied on for navigational guidance. You will need to bring a map and compass on all upland routes, and know how to use them. In bad weather particularly, solid navigational skills are a prerequisite for Irish hill walking.

The terrain underfoot varies from route to route. The Mournes and the eastern Antrim Hills typically offer well drained ground topped by short heather or grass. The Sperrins and the Fermanagh uplands are covered by a thick blanket of peat and can be rather boggy in places. Even lowland routes can be rough and you will need a pair of decent walking boots for all excursions unless the route description says otherwise.

ACCESS

The vast majority of land in Northern Ireland is privately owned and the public has no automatic right of access. Some recognised rights of way do exist but these aren't as numerous or as well protected in law as in many other European countries.

Generally speaking, Northern Irish walks fall into three categories: firstly there are the informal routes that cross private land but where landowners are happy to tolerate public access. The upland routes in the Sperrins fall into this category. Walking in such areas is often dependent on the goodwill of local farmers, and visitors should do everything in their power to comply with the wishes of the owner. Secondly there are the areas owned by bodies such as the Forestry Service, the Environment and Heritage Service or the National Trust. Secure access is one of the benefits of such ownership, and many of the region's best walks now lie within the protective borders of country parks or conservation reserves. The Mourne Mountains are perhaps the most significant area of this type. The vast majority of the range is owned by the Water Service, and walkers have enjoyed unhindered access for decades. There are also plans to formalise the arrangement by designating the Mournes as Northern Ireland's first national park. Finally there's the Waymarked Ways, a collection of formal walking routes where public access has been secured from relevant landowners. Before 2002, Northern Ireland had one, single waymarked route known as the Ulster Way, which extended for 900km and included cross-border sections in the Republic of Ireland. In practical terms the route turned out to be something of a white elephant and in 2002 the concept was abandoned in favour of a series of shorter routes. The new routes are still of varying character and quality but they at least have the advantage of being signposted throughout. This book also includes a selection of the best way-marked walking in the region.

CLIMATE

Northern Ireland, like Ireland as a whole, has notoriously changeable weather. Though this means you have to carry bad-weather clothing even on apparently sunny days, the rapid movement of fresh air brings its own pleasures.

The proximity of the Atlantic Gulf Stream ensures a relatively mild climate all year round, with the prevailing winds coming from the west or southwest. Most rain falls as soon the clouds meet land, allowing the east to enjoy a dryer climate. Nonetheless, it is advisable to be prepared for showers throughout the region at all times of the year.

The warmest months are July and August, when daily temperatures range between 16°C and 24°C. Walking isn't restricted to the summer, however, and many of the best outdoor experiences can be had on crisp, clear days in autumn, winter or spring.

The coldest months are January and February, and the mountains are generally covered by snow several times during this period. The snow rarely lasts more than a couple of days before thawing, however, and lowland areas receive just one or two modest falls each year. Winter daytime temperatures range from 0°C to 4°C, while night time temperatures usually drop below freezing. This is low enough to freeze upland bog, and it's a great time to tackle the region's wetter walking routes. It's a wonderful feeling to skip across the surface of frozen turf knowing you would be sinking knee-deep at any other time of the year.

Wind chill is perhaps the biggest danger to walkers in winter. The combination of low temperatures and strong winds can catch people out, especially on mountain routes. As a rule the air temperature drops 2-3°C for every 300m of height gained. Add even a moderate wind chill factor and it soon becomes obvious that several layers of insulation might be needed to keep warm.

Besides the weather, the other seasonal consideration for walkers is the amount of daylight. In mid December the sun rises around 8.45am and sets at 4pm, giving just seven hours of daylight. If you want to complete a long mountain circuit at this time of the year, there's no choice but to start and finish in the dark. By mid June, the sun doesn't set until

10pm and there are seventeen hours of daylight. It's quite possible to start an eight-hour walk at lunchtime and still finish with daylight to spare.

MAPS

Northern Ireland is covered by the Ordnance Survey of Northern Ireland (OSNI) 1:50,000 Discoverer series. The general quality and accuracy of the mapping is very high and the series is the standard reference for all outdoor enthusiasts. The Mourne Mountains in County Down and Lough Erne in County Fermanagh are the only areas covered by smaller scale mapping, with individual sheets published by the OSNI at 1:25,000.

Maps are widely available in local outlets such as outdoor gear shops, tourist offices, bookshops and some newsagents. To purchase maps outside the region, contact the National Map Centre of Ireland (see facing page for contact details).

USEFUL CONTACTS

There are a number of service providers whose contact details might be of assistance to walkers:
Emergencies: Dial 999 for all emergency rescue services, including mountain rescue and coastguard.

Weather: The BBC provides a five day online weather forecast for Northern Ireland at www.bbc.co.uk/weather/ukweather/nireland. A regional telephone forecast is also available from the Meteorological Office on 09014 722 077. Calls cost 60p per minute.

Maps: To purchase OSNI maps outside the region, contact the National Map Centre of Ireland on: +353 (0)1 4760 471, www.irishmaps.ie.

Transport: Bus and train services in Northern Ireland are run by Translink. For full timetable information, contact: 028 9066 6630; www.translink.co.uk.

National Trust Several routes in this book visit property owned by the National Trust. For more information on each reserve, including opening times and charges, contact: 028 9751 0721; www.ntni.org.uk.

Forest Service: Northern Ireland's forest parks are overseen by the Forest Service. For information about park facilities, walking trails and opening times, contact: 028 9052 4480; www.forestserviceni.gov.uk.

Environment & Heritage Service: Several walks in this guide take place in designated country parks. For a more details about each park, contact: 028

9054 6556; www.ehsni.gov.uk/places/parks/parks.shtml.
Waymarked Ways: Seven of the routes touch on Northern Ireland's network of waymarked ways. Each waymarked route has its own leaflet guide which is available from local tourist offices or from: 028 9030 3930; www.waymarkedways.com.
Tourist Information: Tourist Offices can be found in every town or village of significant size in Northern Ireland. Alternatively, contact the Northern Ireland Tourist Board at: Belfast Welcome Centre, 47 Donegall Place, Belfast, BT1 5AU; 028 9024 6609; www.discovernorthernireland.com.

Using This Guide

This guide consists of 34 route descriptions for one-day walks in Northern Ireland. All routes were researched or checked during the summer of 2005 and descriptions were correct at that time.

The routes are organised in a rough north-south format, starting with Rathlin Island off the County Antrim coast and finishing with the southern Mournes. Some of the walks are accessible by public transport but you'll need your own car for many of the more remote excursions. The vast majority are circular in format, and there is just one linear route that demands two cars or a designated driver.

The guide includes a wide variety of routes and offers options to suit every sort of walker. Roughly half the routes are hill walks, while the remainder are lower woodland or coastal excursions. The hope is that such diversity cannot be a bad thing; even the most dedicated hillwalker requires easier outings if the cloud is down or if they want to take the family out for a day. Many of the descriptions also include suggestions for extending the route if desired.

Almost all the walking takes place across open ground or along footpaths. Road walking has been kept to a bare minimum and main roads are avoided altogether. The best walks have been described in each part of the region, with route quality and scenic diversity being the main criteria for inclusion.

GRADING

Grades are included for each walk to give an indication of the overall difficulty level. Grades range from 1 for the easiest walks to 5 for the hardest. The figures are intended as a general guide only – many experienced walkers will be able to draw their own conclusions from the route statistics and written descriptions. None of the routes involve any technical difficulties that would necessitate the use of scrambling or rock climbing skills.

Grade 1: Relatively short walks on well-graded, maintained paths. Surfaces are largely firm underfoot and little ascent or descent is involved. Routes are generally signposted. No serious navigational difficulties.

Grade 2: Routes still follow paths, but these might not be maintained or signposted. Some sections may cross rougher ground or open countryside. There is no sustained ascent or descent but routes can be fairly long. No serious navigational difficulties.

Grade 3: Walks in this category may involve up to 500m of vertical ascent. Terrain can be rough under-foot and any paths are informal in character. Navigation skills are required but route finding is relatively straightforward in good conditions. Most of the region's easy hill walks fall into this category.

Grade 4: Longer mountain excursions involving up to 850m of ascent. Ground can be very rough underfoot and any paths are informal in character. Navigational skills are required throughout and it may be neces-sary to avoid natural hazards such as cliffs.

Grade 5: The longest, most strenuous hill walks fall into this category. Routes visit multiple summits and may involve 1,100m of ascent. Walks tend to last more than seven hours. Good stamina and solid navigational skills are a prerequisite.

MEASUREMENTS

Distances and heights are given in metres and kilometres throughout the book. Since the OS maps work with the metric system, this tends to be the measurement used by walkers. However a concession has been made to the imperial system in the route summary statistics, where distances are given in miles as well as kilometres.

As a general guide, metres should be multiplied by 3.3 to obtain the number of feet, and kilometres should be multiplied by 0.6 to obtain the number of miles.

Route times are generally given as a range. If you are a fast walker you can expect to finish in the shortest time shown, while slower parties may need the full upper limit. Breaks and rest stops are not calculated as part of the allowance.

SKETCH MAPS

Each walk description is accompanied by a sketch map. This is designed to help you locate the route on the relevant OS map. While it isn't possible to include every geographic detail, the major features of the landscape are marked, along with any smaller points that may help you follow the route. Please note that scales and bearings are indicative rather than precise, and should not be relied on for navigational use. Refer to the route statistics for an accurate summary of the distance and ascent for each walk.

The sketch maps also indicate the relevant

start and finish points. To find the exact position of these points, refer to the section entitled 'Start & Finish'. This offers detailed advice on travelling to and from the walk, and gives full grid references for the start and finish locations.

EQUIPMENT

Boots are required for all walks unless the route description advises otherwise. Another general rule of walking in Northern Ireland is that you should always be prepared for adverse weather. In the mountains especially, warm and waterproof clothing is essential even on an apparently sunny day. Gaiters are advisable for cross-country routes after rain.

It is assumed that the relevant OS map and a compass will be carried on all routes. Where a walk takes place in a country park or similar managed reserve, the park authorities sometimes publish a trail map that is more useful than the OS map for walking purposes. The walk description will alert you if this is the case.

Mobile phone coverage is generally good on high ground in the region but may be less reliable in remote valleys. Don't rely on the fact that you'll be able to get a connection whenever you need it.

RESPONSIBLE WALKING

Many walking routes in Northern Ireland depend on the goodwill of landowners for their existence. In recent years, inconsiderate behaviour by some users has led to access being withdrawn and apparently established routes being lost. Damage to farm fences and walls, sheep-worrying dogs and litter are some of the main reasons why walkers become unpopular. By observing the principles of the country code we all help to ensure the future of walking in the region.

The Northern Ireland Country Code is as follows:

1. Respect the people who live and work in the countryside.
2. Know where you're allowed to go and always comply with a landowner's wishes.
3. Keep to paths across farmland and avoid fields where there are animals.
4. Use gates and stiles to cross fences, hedges and walls. If you must climb a gate because it's difficult to open, always do so at the hinged end.
5. Leave gates open or closed as you find them.
6. Don't interfere with livestock, machinery or

crops and pay attention to warning signs.

7. Keep dogs under control. Some routes across farmland have a complete ban on walking with your dog.

8. Protect wildlife, plants and trees and leave all natural places as you find them.

9. Keep all water sources clean.

10. Take your litter home.

11. Guard against risk of fire.

12. Make no unnecessary noise.

13. Respect other recreational users.

14. Take special care on country roads. Walkers should proceed in single file and drivers should reduce their speed. Avoid blocking entrances and gateways when parking.

15. Consider your personal safety. Wear suitable clothing and footwear and don't go out if the weather conditions are beyond your experience.

ROUTE 1:
COUNTY ANTRIM – COASTAL WALK
RATHLIN ISLAND

Follow quiet lanes and cliff-top paths to Northern Ireland's premier seabird site.

Grade: 2
Time: 4-5 hours
Distance: 14.5km (9 miles)
Ascent: 220m (720ft)
Map: OSNI 1:50,000 sheet 5.
Start & Finish: The route starts and finishes at Rathlin Island ferry pier (grid reference: D147510). Ferry services to the island run several times daily from Ballycastle. To check crossing times and conditions, contact Caledonian MacBrayne on: 028 2076 9299.

INTRODUCTION
Rathlin is the largest island off the coast of Northern Ireland. Situated 10km across the Atlantic from Ballycastle, it makes a wonderful place for a walk.

The sheer cliffs and dramatic sea stacks of Kebble National Nature Reserve are the focal point of walking on the island. Situated at the island's western tip, the reserve supports the largest seabird colony in Northern Ireland. From late April to early August the cliffs around West Lighthouse are alive with hundreds of thousands of breading birds. Guillemots, kittiwakes, razorbills, fulmars and puffins can all be seen from the Royal Society for the Protection of Birds (RSPB) viewing platform, where friendly staff are on hand to answer your bird-related questions. The site is generally open during the breeding season but walkers are advised to contact the warden before travelling on: 028 2076 3948.

The reserve itself is situated at the end of a 4km of road. The narrow lane carries little traffic and the route is described to include this section of tarmac. There are alternatives if you want to avoid the road walk, however. During the summer, a minibus service runs from the harbour to the lighthouse, and bicycles are also available for hire. Allow $1^1/_2$-2 hours to complete the cliff-top circuit on its own.

THE ROUTE

From the ferry pier, walk inland to the harbour road. Turn left and follow the road for 300m, then turn right beside a church. Climb along a narrow lane to a junction in front of the island's other church. Turn left here and join the road that runs to the western end of the island.

A memorial plaque near the start of the road commemorates the 500 inhabitants of Rathlin who emigrated during the Great Famine of 1845-1851. As you continue there are fine views south to Fair Head on the mainland. The buoy in the middle of Church Bay indicates the spot where *HMS Drake*, a 14,000-ton battleship, sank after being torpedoed in 1917. There are more than 40 such wrecks in the waters around Rathlin, which makes it a popular spot with divers.

Continue west along the lane, keeping to the main road at several junctions. Roughly one hour of walking will bring you to the gate that marks the boundary of Kebble National Nature Reserve. The road now turns into a gravel track underfoot.

Around 100m beyond the entrance to the reserve, turn left off the track. Follow a footpath

<u>Route 1</u>

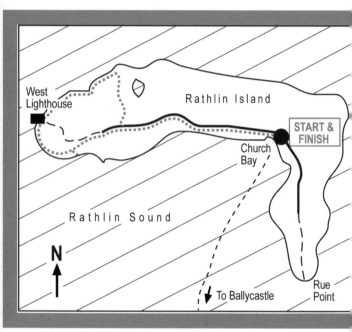

·········· Route Described

through the grass to a red metal gate. For a short detour, go through this gate and follow the faint path to the top of a concrete stairway. The steps descend steeply down a cliff face to a small pier at Cooraghy Bay. Incredibly, this path was used to transport all the materials to build West Lighthouse. Work could only progress in favourable weather conditions, and after three years of effort the lighthouse was finally finished in 1917.

Return to the red gate and turn left. Cross a field, pass through a wooden gate, and continue to the cliff edge. The path now undulates along the top of the steep basalt cliffs, which share a volcanic history with much of the Causeway Coast to the south. The seabirds become more numerous as you progress and you'll need to cross several stiles before reaching the lighthouse.

The path to the lighthouse is only open when the warden is in attendance. If this is the case, turn left down a flight of concrete steps. One of three lighthouses on Rathlin, West Lighthouse is unusual because its beacon is situated halfway down the cliff to avoid the mists that gather above. The RSPB viewing platform is located beside the building and free binoculars are available for a closer look at the birds on the stacks and escarpments to the north.

Return to the top of the slope and turn left, now heading northeast around the cliffs. This side of the headland provides more dramatic coastal scenery, and fine views northeast to Scotland. Pass a small waterfall at the edge of Kinramer Wood and continue east between the cliffs and the trees.

The cliff section ends when you reach the fence marking the eastern boundary of the woodland. Savour the final views northeast over Lack Point and turn right along the fence. Cross rough ground beside the wood to reach the road. Turn left onto the tarmac and retrace your initial steps back to the harbour.

COUNTY ANTRIM – COASTAL WALK
NORTH ANTRIM CLIFF PATH

A magnificent linear route along the most celebrated stretch of coastline in Northern Ireland.

Grade: 2
Time: 5–6 hours
Distance: 15km (9½ miles)
Ascent: 200m (660ft)
Map: OSNI 1:50,000 sheet 5.
Start & Finish: The route starts at the parking area for Carrick-a-Rede rope bridge (grid reference: D052448). The site is signed from the B12 just east of Ballintoy. The walk finishes at the car park for the Giant's Causeway (grid reference: C945439). The causeway is situated along the B146, around 3km north of Bushmills.

INTRODUCTION

This varied and highly enjoyable coastal route explores Ireland's only World Heritage Area. The most famous feature of the walk is the Giant's

Causeway, where 40,000 hexagonal stones jut into the Atlantic. The site is not the only attraction of the area, however – far from it. In fact the whole of the Causeway Coast is so striking it is protected as an Area of Outstanding Natural Beauty.

A 52km waymarked path called the Causeway Coast Way runs along the coast from Portstewart to Ballycastle. Here we describe the best one-day section of that path, starting at the thrilling Carrick-a-Rede rope bridge. The route then traces the shoreline past sandy beaches, secluded harbours and sheer cliff tops to finish at the Giant's Causeway.

Despite its linear format, return transport is not a problem. The area has a well developed tourism infrastructure, which includes the Causeway Rambler bus service. This frequent summer shuttle is run by Ulsterbus and provides an easy way of linking the walk's start and the finish points. At other times of the year the Antrim Coaster serves the area.

A marked path is followed throughout and stiles are in place wherever necessary. The shoreline around Ballintoy and Portbradden may not be passable at very high tides, however, so check the water levels before you walk. There is a charge for visiting the Carrick-a-Rede rope bridge at the start and for parking at the Giant's Causeway at the end.

THE ROUTE

If you want to visit Carrick-a-Rede rope bridge, pay your dues at the turnstile and follow the well-benched path east from the car park. This initial side trip adds a further 2km to the day's total. The bridge has been raised every summer for over 250 years to allow fishermen to access their nets. The island juts into a salmon migration route, giving rise to the name Carrig-a-Rade, or 'the rock in the road'.

Return to the car park and begin the route itself. Follow the obvious path west along the top of the cliffs. Rathlin Island lies 7km northwest across the sea and on a clear day the Mull of Kintyre in Scotland is also visible on the horizon. Round the top of Boheeshane Bay, join a minor road and descend to Ballintoy harbour. This quiet, picturesque harbour is protected by a natural outer breakwater. An adjacent tearoom offers refreshments.

Cross the car park at the back of the harbour. Where the tarmac peters out, a footpath takes over. Trace the shoreline west past a series of stacks and islands, crossing a couple of stiles along

Route 2

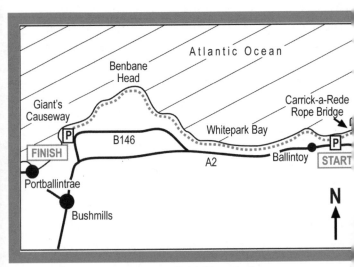

.... Route Described

the way. You then cross onto the top of a stone beach and skirt around the base of a cliff. A boulder hop leads around the corner to the long sandy sweep of Whitepark Bay.

Cross the beach to the cliffs at its western end. Nestled beneath the rock is Portbradden, an idyllic collection of houses fronted by a small harbour. You'll have to cross more boulders at the back of the beach to reach the hamlet itself. St Gobban's Church lies beside the second house; it is no larger than a garden shed and holds the accolade of the smallest church in Ireland.

Continue through a natural rock arch and follow the path round Gid Point, crossing a mixture of rock and grass as you trace the indented coastline to Dunseverick. Several more stiles need to be crossed on this 2km stretch, which ends at the ruins of the sixteenth-century Dunseverick Castle.

The grassy path continues northwest from Dunseverick, climbing towards Benbane Head and the highest part of the route. You are now tracing the cliff line some 100m above the ocean. The path undulates past Hamilton's Seat, where there are wonderful views along the rugged coastline to the Giant's Causeway some 4km west.

Midway between Hamilton's Seat and the causeway you come to Plaskin Head. Just west of here, beyond two narrow fingers of rock, lies the wreck of the *Girona*, perhaps the most famous ship of the ill-fated Spanish Armada.

It is not long now before you arrive at the Giant's Causeway. If you don't want to visit the site itself, continue along the cliff path to the visitor centre. Alternatively, a steep descent down the Shepherd's Steps will bring you to the basalt columns at the shore. Legend dictates that the Irish giant, Finn MacCumhaill, built the causeway as part of a bridge over to Scotland. Unfortunately, scientists maintain the hexagonal structures were created by cooling lava flows around 60 million years ago.

To finish, follow the 1km-long tarmac lane from the site to the visitor centre, situated at the top of the hill to the west.

ROUTE 3:
COUNTY ANTRIM – COASTAL WALK
FAIR HEAD & MURLOUGH BAY

*Two short coastal circuits explore a beautiful bay
and the tallest sea cliffs in Northern Ireland.*

Grade: 2
Time: 3¹/₂–4¹/₂ hours
Distance: 13km (8 miles)
Ascent: 440m (1445ft)
Map: OSNI 1:50,000 sheet 5.
Start & Finish: The route starts and finishes at a
parking area at the top of Murlough Bay (grid ref-
erence: D191418). The area is generally accessed
via the A2 Ballycastle-Cushendun road. Turn east
off the road in Ballyvoy and follow signs for Torr
Head. Murlough Bay is signed north off the Torr
Head road after roughly 4km. The car park is
marked by a National Trust information board.

INTRODUCTION
The tallest sea cliffs in Northern Ireland lie at the
northeastern corner of the region, where a 4km

stretch of basalt escarpment rises to a height of 186m. Sharing a volcanic history and hexagonal form with the nearby Giant's Causeway, the cliffs of Fair Head are one of the toughest rock climbing venues in the British Isles.

For walkers, the lofty plateau above the cliffs provides a wonderful vantage point for Rathlin Island and the Scottish coast. At the eastern end of the headland the precipice relents slightly to allow access to the enclosed cove of Murlough Bay. The natural grandeur of the scenery makes this one of the most beautiful spots in the province, and much of the area is now owned by the National Trust.

Two short walks are described here, one around Murlough Bay (6km) and one along the cliffs at Fair Head (7km). If you only have time for one route the Murlough Bay loop offers more variety, but the best option is to link the circuits together and make a figure-of-eight route of 13km.

The routes spend most of their time on small footpaths or tracks. The Murlough Bay walk involves a steep descent and ascent, while the Fair Head loop is undulating and largely waymarked. Both routes include sections along the top of sheer cliffs so make sure to take care near the edge.

THE ROUTE
Murlough Bay Loop

From the top car park, follow the narrow road downhill towards Murlough Bay. Pass a white house and the first of several old lime kilns. Chalk was once burnt in these kilns to produce lime, which was spread on the fields to reduce the acidity of the soil.

Continue to the middle parking area, situated at the apex of a hairpin bend. Two map boards label the parts of Scotland that can be seen on the horizon, from the Mull of Kintyre to the Paps of Jura.

Turn left at the parking area and join a gravel track. Descend diagonally across the slope, heading towards the imposing cliffs of Fair Head. Continue to the end of the track beneath a jumble of boulders. Here, at the bottom of the cliffs on the left, you will find two low tunnels that mark the entrance to an abandoned coal mine.

Retrace your steps along the track for 100m and turn left onto a grassy footpath. Follow the path past two ruined miner's cottages to reach a stony cove. Now continue along the shoreline, heading to the left of a rocky hummock. Here the

Route 3

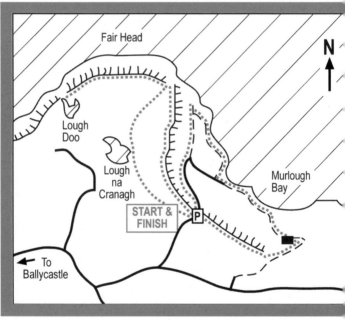

·········· Route Described

path consolidates into a track again and leads you to the road near the bottom parking area.

Turn left and follow the road to a gate. Pass through the gate and immediately on the right you'll see a small white cottage marked 'bothy'. Turn right onto a narrow footpath just past the cottage, with the junction marked by a wooden post. The path climbs steeply into the woodland above the bay, passing through thick swathes of bluebells in the spring.

Cross a stile and stream and continue to Benvan Farmhouse, where there are wonderful views across Murlough Bay. Join a track behind the farmhouse and climb steeply through a hairpin bend to the top of the slope. Turn right and follow a path along the escarpment to return to the top car park.

Fair Head Loop

Start at the information board at the top car park and join a path that leads northwest around the right side of a fence. Yellow paint splashes on the rocks mark the way.

The path is often indistinct but the simple instruction is to keep following the edge of the cliffs. Climb across several undulations to reach the top of the Grey Man's Path, a chasm-like gully that climbers use to reach the base of the cliffs.

Continue past the gully and round the tip of the headland to Lough Doo. Another gully heads down the cliffs beneath the lough, offering an easier descent if you want to visit the impressive amphitheatre of crags below and view some of the hardest rock climbs in the country.

Return to Lough Doo and retrace your steps along the cliffs to Grey Man's Path. Near this gully, turn right and join a path that descends south towards Lough na Cranagh. The prominent island in the middle of the lough is a fine example of a *crannóg*, a small Neolithic settlement built in a lake for defensive reasons and once accessed via a hidden causeway.

Continue along the eastern side of the lough to reach the hamlet of Coolanlough. From here, follow the path and the paint splashes and climb gradually southeast back to the car park.

ROUTE 4:
COUNTY ANTRIM — HILL WALK
TROSTAN & THE MOYLE WAY

A linear route over rough mountain terrain to the highest point in County Antrim.

Grade: 3
Time: 4^1/$_2$-5^1/$_2$ hours
Distance: 14km (8^1/$_2$ miles)
Ascent: 515m (1675ft)
Maps: OSNI 1:50,000 sheets 9 and 5.
Start & Finish: The route starts at a parking lay-by 60m east of the main entrance for Glenariff Forest Park (grid reference: D202207). The lay-by is located on the A43 Cushendall-Ballymena road, around 9km south of Cushendall and 20km north of Ballmena.

The route ends at Orra Beg parking area (grid reference: D144277). The lay-by is marked by a route information board and is located beside a stone bridge on a minor road between Cushendall and Armoy.

INTRODUCTION

This route follows the southern part of the Moyle Way across a mixture of forest tracks and rough upland moor. The highlight of the trip is a visit to Trostan, Antrim's highest summit at 550m.

After the ascent of Trostan, the route continues north over Slieveanorra (508m). The northeastern slopes of this mountain played a prominent role in local history when they became the site of the Battle of Orra in 1559. During the battle, the Macdonnell clan covered the ground with rushes to make it appear solid. Members of the Maquillan and O'Neill clans were tricked and floundered into chest-deep bog, only to be slaughtered as they tried to struggle free.

The route crosses unimproved moorland that can be both wet and rough underfoot. The intermittent waymarking posts of the Moyle Way are followed throughout, with the exception of the 1km detour to the summit of Trostan. Despite the signposts, the wild, featureless terrain means full navigation skills are required in bad weather.

Unfortunately the remote location and linear format of the route mean it's only feasible if you have two vehicles or a designated driver. To extend the walk, consider adding the next 9km section of the Moyle Way, which continues north from Orra Beg through forest and along a small stream to finish at Breen Bridge on the B15.

The Route

From the lay-by, walk 60m west along the road to reach a gravel track on the right. Pass a metal gate and head up the track into mixed woodland. Roughly 250m later, turn left at a junction. Climb gradually through the partially cleared plantation and turn left again after 1km. Follow this track to a stone road bridge over the Essathohan Burn.

Cross the road and join a small, grassy footpath that heads northwest between the forest and the river. You pass a waterfall on the left before arriving at a track over another old stone bridge.

Waymarking may be rather sporadic over the next section so take care not to lose the path. Cross the track and continue straight ahead along a fire-break in the trees. After 50m turn left and cross a stream. Turn immediately right on the opposite bank and follow a path upstream through thick trees. The path crosses the stream several

<u>Route 4</u>

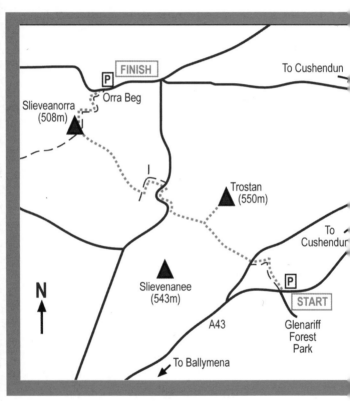

·········· Route Described

times before climbing beside another small water-fall to a clearing.

Cross the clearing and head into the trees again, still following the line of the stream. After roughly 200m, leave the stream and follow the path left through the trees. Pick your way over the roots and branches to reach the edge of the plantation.

Once you've emerged into the open, continue straight ahead over rough ground. Climb to the corner of the forest, then turn left along the top of the trees. After 200m veer away from the planta-tion to the right, now heading north over the open mountainside.

The waymarkers become more frequent as you climb over rough tussock grass on the southwest-ern shoulder of Trostan. At the top of the shoulder you meet a fence. If you want to detour to the highest point in Antrim, turn right here and follow the fence uphill. Head towards two stone cairns on top of a rise, then cross a stile and continue across bare, rocky ground to the trig point at the summit. Wide-ranging views include all the Antrim Hills and much of Northern Ireland's northeast coast.

Retrace your steps along the fence and return to the waymarked route. Turn right and cross the fence. Across the valley the masts at the top of Slieveanorra mark your next destination.

Descend west over sometimes wet ground and cross a wooden footbridge over the Glendun River. A short climb now brings you to a minor road. Turn right and follow the tarmac into the forest. After roughly 1km, turn left onto a gravel forest track. Turn left again at a T-junction and continue for a further 600m to a wooden footbridge on the right.

Cross the footbridge and head along a fire-break to open ground. Here you join a rough and occasionally wet track that climbs past a small copse of pines to the top of Slieveanorra.

At the summit, turn right along a gravel track. Pass between the two communication masts, where there are good views north over the solitary cone of Knocklayd. Follow the track as it descends northeast through several switchbacks to Slieveanorra Forest. Continue through the trees to the road and parking area at Orra Beg.

ROUTE 5:
COUNTY ANTRIM — WOODLAND/HILL WALK
GLENARIFF FOREST PARK

A varied circuit with an optional detour away from the forest trails to a scenic mountain summit.

Grade: 1–2
Time: 2½–3 hours
Distance: 8km (5 miles)
Ascent: 310m (1020ft)
Map: OSNI 1:50,000 sheet 9.
Start & Finish: The circuit starts and finishes at Manor Lodge car park, on the eastern side of Glenariff Forest Park (grid reference: J344325). The park itself is located along the A43 Ballymena-Cushendall road. Turn south off the road around 2.5km east of the main entrance to Glenariff Forest, onto a road signed for Manor Lodge. The car park is situated at the end of the road around 1.5km later.

Route 5

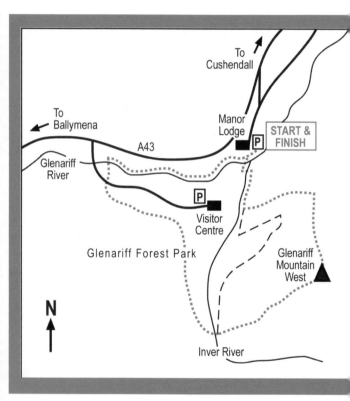

·········· Route Described

INTRODUCTION

Glenariff is known as the queen of the Antrim Glens. Thackeray called it 'a Switzerland in Miniature', no doubt inspired by its forests, rivers and steep glacial escarpments.

This route explores the waterfalls and woodland of Glenariff Forest Park. The 12km² park covers the lower slopes on both sides of the valley but the main recreational interest lies in the southern section. Here the rocky gorges and fast-flowing waters of the Inver and Glenariff rivers provide the park's main attraction. Some 22 waterfalls are passed in the first kilometre of this route alone.

The park contains four waymarked walking trails between 1km and 9km long. This route combines the blue Waterfall Trail and the red Scenic Trail, following maintained paths throughout. For more adventurous types we also describe an optional detour to the summit of Glenariff Mountain West (350m). The side trip is unsigned and crosses rough mountain terrain but allows wonderful views across the Glenariff Valley.

There is an admission charge for both vehicles and pedestrians entering the park. You will be given a small-scale trail map when you arrive, which is a useful addition to the OS map.

THE ROUTE

The sound of rushing water can be heard from the car park even before you start the walk. In a forested ravine beside Manor Lodge, the Glenariff River thunders down to meet the Inver River. Through the trees you can just make out the last big waterfall on the Inver.

Walk around the back of the lodge and join a path that runs along the wooded bank of the Glenariff River. Pass a turnstile at the park boundary and continue straight ahead. Ignore a bridge on the left; you will return this way at the end of the circuit.

Follow the turbulent water upstream past numerous small falls. The rock walls soon draw closer and the path takes to a wooden walkway built into the cliff. This dark, moist gorge is a haven for many species of fern, moss and liverwort, and has been designated a National Nature Reserve. At the head of the ravine lies perhaps the most famous waterfall in the Glens of Antrim, the powerful, double drop of Ess-na-Larach, meaning 'the Mare's Fall'.

Follow the walkway across the river beneath Ess-na-Larach. The path continues upstream through more open woodland, passing several minor cascades. Follow the blue waymarkers through a junction and cross another bridge to arrive at Hermit's Fall. Cross the river again at a third bridge and pick up the red waymarkers of the Scenic Trail on the opposite bank.

A short detour along the path to the left will bring you to the visitor's centre, where displays highlight the history and ecology of the area. To continue on the route, follow the red Scenic Trail away from the river. Cross a tarmac road and climb through the pines to a large clearing with views down the length of Glenariff. In summer the clearing is covered by swathes of Purple Loosestrife.

The path now undulates towards the upper reaches of the Inver River. As you cross the river you have a choice of two routes.

To stay within the forest boundary, keep on the main path and continue to follow the red waymarkers. Wind down through several switchbacks to the bottom of the slope and cross the bridge over the Inver. Turn right and cross the Glenariff, then turn right again to return to Manor Lodge.

To leave the forest and explore the escarpments to the east, look out for a small stile on your right just after you cross the upper Inver. Cross the stile and climb east along the boundary of the forest, crossing rough moorland underfoot. At the corner of the plantation, negotiate a stretch of boggy ground and climb over several rocky hummocks to the top of Glenariff Mountain West.

Cross the rounded summit and head for Loughnacarry, on the northern side of the mountain. Locate Doon Burn, the lough's outlet stream, and follow the watercourse north. Before long you arrive at a lookout point where you can appreciate the full grandeur of the escarpments on the northern side of Glenariff.

Descend along the stream to an old mine track, which zigzags steeply down to the embankment of a former railway. Here you meet another, more prominent track. Turn left here and follow the track back towards the forest.

Pass through a gate at the forest boundary and turn right to rejoin the red trail. Cross the bridges over the Inver and Glenariff rivers, then turn right and return to Manor Lodge.

ROUTE 6:
COUNTY ANTRIM — HILL WALK
SHANE'S HILL TO GLENARM

A scenic linear route along a high coastal plateau in the Glens of Antrim.

Grade: 3
Time: 5-6 hours
Distance: 21km (13 miles)
Ascent: 480m (1575ft)
Map: OSNI 1:50,000 sheet 9.
Start & Finish: The route starts from a car park in Ballyboley Forest on Shane's Hill (grid reference: J314992). The car park is situated on the southern side of the A36 Larne-Ballymena road, around 10km west of Larne and 21km east of Ballymena.

The route ends in Glenarm village, on the A2 Larne-Carnlough road.

INTRODUCTION
This is one of the most enjoyable upland routes in the Antrim Hills, with firm terrain, dramatic natural landforms and fantastic views from start to finish.

The route begins with an ascent of Agnew's Hill (474m), then heads north across a series of summits between 300m and 400m high. The hills rise gently to the west but fall away steeply to the east, which suggests the glaciers of the last ice age ran parallel to the shore. The most striking formation is Sallagh Braes, a semi-circular basalt escarpment that has been designated an Area of Special Scientific Interest. The amphitheatre was created when ice cut into unstable slopes and caused a massive land slip, leaving the vertical cliffs 2km long and 100m high that are visible today.

The walk follows part of the two-day Antrim Hills Way, which has superseded the old Ulster Way in this area. This means your progress is eased by frequent stiles and waymarking posts, and route finding is a relatively simple affair in good conditions. However, much of the time is spent on faint paths across open terrain and navigation skills are required in bad weather.

If you have two vehicles, it is possible to avoid the final 3km of tarmac by parking on wide verges on the road above Glenarm. If not, consider taking the Glenarm-Larne and Larne-Ballymena buses to transport yourself between start and finish.

The Route

From Shane's Hill car park, cross the road and join a grassy footpath beside a route signpost. Follow the path along a fire-break in the forest and cross a stile to open mountainous terrain.

The cairn that marks the southern summit of Agnew's Hill is now visible to the northeast. Head directly towards the cairn, climbing gradually over rough tussock grass. Cross two tracks and a stile to reach the summit itself. At the top, you are rewarded with your first real views, which include the Belfast Hills, the Mourne Mountains, the Sperrins and Scotland. It's a wonderful panorama and one that stays with you for the duration of the route.

Turn left at the cairn and descend slightly, then begin the steady ascent to the higher, northern peak. Cross the broad ridge to the summit cairn at the far edge of the plateau. This is the highest point of the route, and the remainder of the walk can now be seen stretching away to the north.

Descend along the marker posts to a stile, then turn right beside a fence. Short grass provides an easier walking surface as you drop down to meet a road. Turn right along the tarmac, where there are

<u>Route 6</u>

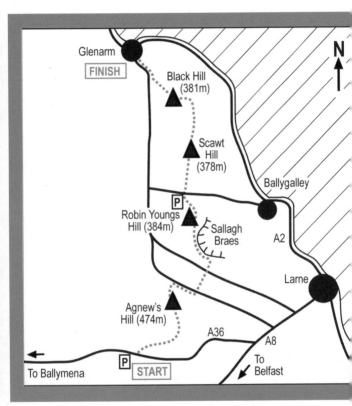

.... Route Described

good views back across the cliffs of Agnew's Hill.

After almost 1km, turn left off the road and cross another stile. Follow the path over a field and cross a stream above an artificial lough. Here you join a grass track between high stone walls. Negotiate several wooden gates and a stream to reach another minor road.

Turn left along the tarmac for 120m then cross into a field on the right. A series of stiles leads across the fields to heathery ground above Sallagh Braes. Follow a fence around the lip of the escarpment, with gullies allowing the occasional glimpse into the void below. The airy sensation and the view over the curving cliffs make this a memorable piece of walking.

The path veers away from the edge to climb over the shoulder of Robin Young's Hill. You then descend northwest over a short section of stony track and more cropped grass to a car park.

Cross the road and climb along the right side of a field to the summit of Ballycoos. A gradual descent and ascent then brings you to Scawt Hill. Continue in the same vein across a series of grassy undulations, keeping to the high ground near the eastern edge of the plateau. The coastal views remain impressive throughout, with the rocky outcrops of the Maidens or Hulin Rocks visible out to sea.

The path eventually swings west across rougher ground to reach the trig point at the summit of Black Hill. This marks the start of a diagonal descent northwest off the plateau. Follow the marker posts down through the fields and across several rocky hummocks. Eventually you meet a stone wall at the right side of a field and descend through gorse bushes to a road.

Turn right along the road and follow the tarmac for almost 2km, then turn left onto a smaller road. You arrive at the top of Altmore Street in Glenarm village roughly 1km later.

COUNTY DERRY – HILL WALK
BINEVENAGH CLIFFS

*Explore the cliffs and pinnacles of one of the most
unusual landscapes in the north.*

Grade: 2
Time: 2-2½ hours
Distance: 6.5km (4 miles)
Ascent: 200m (660ft)
Map: OSNI 1:50,000 sheet 4.
Start & Finish: The circuit starts and finishes at the
car park beside Binevenagh Lake, at the top of the
cliffs (grid reference: C691308). The area is generally approached via Limavady to the south. From
there, take the A2 north to Artikelly and continue
east on the B201 to Coleraine. Two kilometres east
of Artikelly, turn left and begin to climb towards
Binevenagh Mountain. Turn left again after 5km,
following signs for Binevenagh Forest. The
entrance to the forest is located on the left, 1km
further on. Follow the track to the car park at the
end of the road.

Introduction

The Binevenagh cliffs tower over the Magilligan lowlands of northern County Derry. Cutting into the northern slopes of Binevenagh Mountain, the basalt escarpment has a vertical drop of more than 100m and dominates the landscape for miles around.

The cliffs are unique in Ireland thanks to their geology and ecology. The precipice harbours arctic-alpine and coastal flora, and has been classified an Area of Special Scientific Interest. The rock itself was created by ancient lava flows and invites inevitable comparison with the more famous basalt formations at the Giant's Causeway, 30km away to the east.

The walk makes a circuit around the main escarpment, exploring the rock walls from above and below. Though it's relatively short, the quality of the route means it is recommended for all. Navigation is relatively straightforward – way-marking posts provide initial guidance and stiles are in place throughout. Small, informal paths cover much of the route and part of the old Ulster Way is also followed. However there's no avoiding the fact that half the walk takes place beside a sheer drop. Make sure to exercise due care and attention near the cliff edge.

THE ROUTE

From the car park, head towards the cliffs on the path marked by an Ulster Way post. Keep right at a fork and follow the trail to the cliff edge, where you are met by wonderful views. The flat farmland that stretches beneath you to the spur of Magilligan Point is in fact the largest coastal plain in Ireland. To the east of the point lies the long sandy beach around Benone, while the hills of Inishowen rise beyond Lough Foyle to the west.

Follow the path northeast along the cliff top to another waymarking post at the edge of the forest. You will need to take care here to choose the right path. Resist the temptation to follow the obvious trail into the forest – fallen trees have blocked this route. Keep left instead and continue along the very edge of the escarpment, descending a narrow strip of grass between the forest and cliff. Though it seems little travelled, this is actually the line of the old Ulster Way.

Follow the path into the trees beside another waymarking post and begin to zigzag down

Route 7

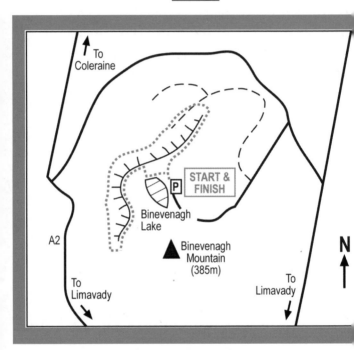

To
Coleraine

START &
FINISH

Binevenagh
Lake

A2

Binevenagh
Mountain
(385m)

To
Limavady

To
Limavady

N

·········· Route Described

through the forest. The terrain becomes steeper as you descend and the ground can be muddy after rain.

At the bottom of the slope, join a gravel vehicle track and turn left. When the track comes to an end, continue ahead on a small footpath and cross a stile beside a metal gate. You are now out into the open, directly beneath the Binevenagh cliffs.

Follow a faint path along the right-hand side of the field. When the trees fall away to your right, begin to traverse across the field to the left, climbing very gradually towards the base of the rocky escarpment. Along the way you will need to cross several more fences, each of which is bridged by a wooden stile. The path eventually becomes lost in the grass, though the general line of the route is indicated by the stiles.

Towards the centre of the cliffs a steep gully cuts down the precipice. Beyond this the ground begins to undulate through a series of hummocks. Keep climbing, drawing gradually closer to the base of the cliffs. Two distinct waves of rock now lie to your left, the nearer stacks having broken off the main escarpment.

Continue ahead, now passing between several

sharp hummocks. Eventually you'll see a distinctive tooth of rock lying just beneath the main precipice, with a grassy ramp to its left. The path consolidates again near the base of the ramp and a steady climb brings you to the top of the cliffs.

Veer left as you reach the top of the escarpment and begin to trace the cliff line north. Keep climbing gently over the grassy slope and pass through a metal gate in a fence.

Soon after this the ascent eases and Binevenagh Lake comes into sight ahead. Continue along the edge of the precipice until you are forced right by the lip of a gully. Follow the path to the lake shore and turn left across the concrete outlet dam. A track leads the final few metres back to the car park.

ROUTE 8:
COUNTY DERRY — WATERSIDE WALK
ROE VALLEY COUNTRY PARK

A series of easy riverside paths can be tailored to personal taste in this tranquil country park.

Grade: 1
Time: 2¹/₂–3¹/₂ hours
Distance: 10km (6 miles)
Ascent: 100m (330ft)
Map: OSNI 1:50,000 sheet 7.
Start & Finish: The circuit starts and finishes at the visitor centre in the middle of the Roe Valley Country Park (grid reference: C679202). The park is generally accessed from Limavady, situated 4km north at the junction of the A2 and A37. From the roundabout on the A2 at the western edge of town, head south along the B192 towards Dungiven. The way to the park is marked from this junction, with signs leading directly to the visitor centre.

INTRODUCTION
Roe Valley Country Park lies just south of Limavady

in County Derry. It extends for 5km on either side of the River Roe, and encompasses deciduous woodland, sheer-walled gorges and fast-flowing rapids. The park owes almost all its beauty and character to the river, which derives its name from the Irish *ruadh*, meaning red, after its peat-stained water.

The turbulent river once powered a thriving linen industry, and also became the basis of a ground-breaking exercise in electricity production. An enterprising local man named John Edward Ritter discovered how to harness the water's energy, and in 1896 Limavady became the first town in Ireland to be powered by hydroelectricity. The visitor centre offers plenty of detail about the valley's past and present, and makes an excellent starting point for exploring the area.

Most of the walks in the park begin along one side of the river, cross the water, and return along the opposite bank. Five bridges mean circular routes can be completed from any of the various parking areas and can be varied in length from a 2km jaunt to a 10km circuit of the entire park. Here we describe the complete circuit in the understanding that it can be shortened to personal taste. The paths are largely flat and well maintained, with the only rough terrain around Carrick Rocks at the southern edge of the park. Boots are recommended in wet conditions.

THE ROUTE

From the front of the visitor centre, turn right and cross a footbridge over the mill stream. Continue straight ahead on a tarmac footpath to reach the river bank. Here the path turns to gravel underfoot and heads upstream, past a meadow and into deciduous woodland.

Continue past a wier to reach a footbridge after 1.5km. Do not cross the bridge but continue along a smaller footpath on the western bank. A brief climb takes you round a bend in the river, then another climb leads into dense woodland high above the water. Pass around the edge of a field to reach the Carrick Rocks parking area.

Turn left beside an information board at the corner of the car park. A flight of steps now leads into the steep-sided Carrick Rocks gorge. Cross a metal footbridge, that is thought to date from 1900, and climb more steps beneath the cliff on the opposite bank. The main path leads to Carrick church but this route veers left on a rough side

Route 8

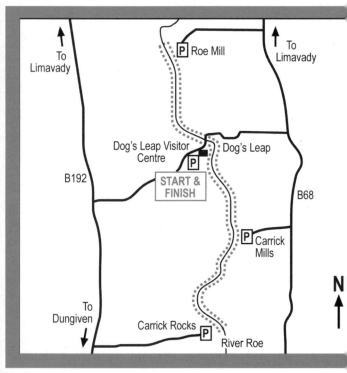

.... Route Described

path and descends back to the river.

You now begin to follow the eastern bank of the river downstream. The path traces the edge of open farmland past a couple of wiers. Shortly after a footbridge you come to a series of old buildings. The Roe Valley was an important linen manufacturing centre between the seventeenth and nineteenth centuries and these are the buildings of the old Scutch Mill, where linen flax was pounded to expose the tough interior fibres.

Beyond the mill, 1.5km of largely flat, tree-lined path brings you to the Dog's Leap. This is the most impressive rapid in the park, where the whole river feeds through a rock channel about 2m wide. The Roe Valley was ruled by the O'Cahan clan for nearly 500 years until 1602, and the rapid was named after one of their hounds who leapt over the gap to deliver warning of an imminent attack.

Continue past the rapid to reach a road bridge. To finish the route here, turn left across the bridge and return to the visitor centre. To continue on the longer route, keep to the eastern bank and cross the road. Pass through a gate and enter an area of mixed woodland that continues to the northern boundary of the park.

The banks become steeper and higher as the river enters a long rocky gorge. The path forks several times along this section; keep to the left at each junction to follow the river. Pass the site of O'Cahan's Castle (now just a mound commanding the river cliffs), then arrive at the lookout of O'Cahan's Rock. A metal footbridge crosses the river beneath the precipice, though this route keeps to the eastern bank.

The terrain becomes flatter again as you weave through thick deciduous woodland towards Roe Mill car park. Keep to the river bank to reach the footbridge that provides the northernmost crossing point in the park.

Cross the river and turn left, now following the path along the western bank. The path leads upstream through woodland for around 1.5km to bring you back to the visitor centre.

ROUTE 9:
COUNTY DERRY — WOODLAND WALK
BANAGHER GLEN & FOREST

Follow a series of tracks past a remote reservoir, an
ancient oak woodland and a forestry plantation.

Grade: 1
Time: 3-4 hours
Distance: 12km (7^1/$_2$ miles)
Ascent: 280m (920ft)
Maps: OSNI 1:50,000 sheets 7 and 8.
Start & Finish: The route starts and finishes at the
Filter House car park at Banagher Glen (grid refer-
ence: C671045). The area is generally reached via
Dungiven and the A6. At the western edge of
Dungiven, turn south onto the B74. The 6km route
to Banagher Glen is signed from the junction. If the
main car park beside the Old Filter House is closed,
alternative parking is available shortly before the
end of the road.

INTRODUCTION
This circuit links two river valleys on the northern

edge of the Sperrin Mountains. It begins by exploring Banagher Glen, a nature reserve that harbours one of the most treasured ancient oak woods in the North. It then climbs across a low ridge covered by pines before finishing along the banks of the Glenedra Water.

The Glenedra marks a return to deciduous vegetation, but local legend has a word of warning for passing walkers. St Patrick banished snakes from Ireland by driving them into the sea, a feat he achieved by first directing them into the rivers. When one particular snake reached the Glenedra Water it was so big it became trapped in a pool. St Patrick imprisoned the massive serpent in the river, where it is reputed to remain to this day.

The other highlight of the route is Altnaheglish Dam and Reservoir. The dam was constructed in the early 1930s to provide a reliable water source for the inhabitants of County Derry. It holds around 500 million gallons of water and is the highest dam in Northern Ireland at 42m.

A series of tarmac lanes and forestry tracks are followed for the duration of the walk, making it suitable for most of the family. The route is not marked, however, so you will need to bring a map.

If you do not want to complete the full circuit, many people walk only as far as the reservoir before retracing their steps to the car park. Allow 1½ hours for this 5km return trip.

THE ROUTE

Follow a footpath southeast from the top corner of the car park. Join a tarmac lane and turn right, beginning to climb uphill. Within 300m you come to a fork in the road. Keep left along the route signed to the dam; you will return along the right-hand fork at the end of the walk.

Cross an old stone bridge over the Glenedra Water and continue to climb steadily. The mixed woodland on either side of the road soon becomes dominated by sessile oak, and the ancient trees provide beautiful surrounds. The woodland eventually falls away and the views become more open, with the steep-sided river valley dropping away to your right.

Around 2.5km from the start the road forks again; keep left and pass over a rise. Altnaheglish Dam and Reservoir now come into view ahead, and you can detour down to visit the dam if you like.

To complete the longer circuit, continue to

Route 9

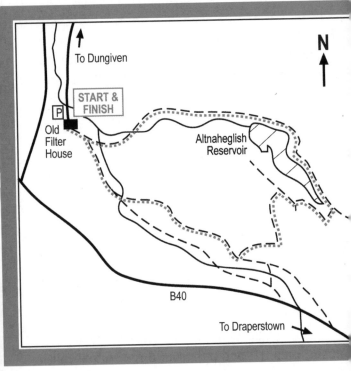

·········· Route Described

follow the lane along the northern shore of the reservoir. Two hundred metres past the dam, branch right onto a smaller vehicle track. This leads to a gate and stile at the edge of Banagher Forest. Cross the stile and follow the track along the banks of the reservoir. The lake is surprisingly long and narrow,and the banks make for pleasant walking.

At the end of the reservoir the track plunges into a dark pine plantation. Turn right shortly after entering the trees and pass over a small bridge with white railings. Follow the track as it swings to the right and begins to climb along the southern side of the water.

Keep right along the main track at the next corner, then turn left at the following junction. A steady ascent brings you to a fire-break at the top of the hill. Continue ahead, with the peak of Mullaghclogha framed between the trees as you descend.

About 1km from the top of the rise you arrive at a T-junction. Turn right here and follow another track that contours along the side of Streeve Mountain. Recent tree felling means that views are wide ranging along this section, and many of the highest peaks of the Sperrins can be seen to the southwest.

The track descends steeply to Glenedra Water. Turn right and cross a bridge that marks the boundary between the forestry plantation and native woodland. A smaller track now follows above the river through a pleasant mixture of hazel, oak and ash.

Around 1km later the track turns to tarmac and arrives at the junction passed at the start of the circuit. Keep left and follow the lane back to the car park.

ROUTE 10:
COUNTY TYRONE — HILL WALK
THE WESTERN SPERRINS

This compact circuit follows quiet roads and open mountainside to the summit of Mullaghcarbatagh.

Grade: 3
Time: 2¹/₂-3¹/₂ hours
Distance: 10km (6 miles)
Ascent: 380m (1250ft)
Map: OSNI 1:50,000 sheet 13.
Start & Finish: The circuit starts and finishes near the bottom of Bradkeel Road, northeast of Plumbridge (grid reference: H495945). From Plumbridge, head north on the B48 towards Dunnamanagh. After 4km you come to a sharp left-hand bend. Turn right at the apex of the bend onto Butterlope Road, which is marked by a low signpost. Continue along Butterlope Road for almost 1km, then turn left onto Bradkeel Road. Around 100m from the junction you'll find space to park a few cars on the right.

INTRODUCTION

This route is a good introduction for walkers new to the Sperrin Mountains. The Sperrins are a range of rounded hills covered by a thick blanket of peat. Rock rarely penetrates the bog and the poorly draining ground can be rough and wet underfoot. Despite its lowly elevation, however, Mullaghcarbatagh (517m) is one of the more enjoyable Sperrin peaks to climb. Apart from Dart Mountain it's perhaps the only summit where you will find any significant outcrops of rock, and its location at the very western edge of the range means it offers superb views into Donegal.

The first half of the route follows deserted roads and tracks along the base of the mountain. You then head north and climb open bog to the summit itself. Solitude is almost guaranteed, though you will need full navigation skills in poor visibility. Archaeology buffs also have the option of starting the route with a visit to Clogherny Wedge Tomb.

To extend the circuit, consider a side trip east from Mullaghcarbatagh to the summit of Mullaghclogher (572m). Allow an extra hour for this 2.5km detour over open mountain terrain.

THE ROUTE

To begin the route with a visit to Clogherny Wedge Tomb, walk back to the junction of Butterlope Road and Bradkeel Road. At the junction a brown signpost indicates the tomb west across old turf cuttings. Follow the wooden marker posts for 500m to reach the site. Inside a circle of eleven schist stones is a single gallery tomb with a large capstone. The site dates from around 2000 BC and was excavated in 1937 by Oliver Davies, who discovered some burnt human bone and a piece of flint arrowhead within the tomb itself.

Retrace your steps to the starting point. Now continue southeast along Bradkeel Road, undulating through an avenue of gorse. After 1km turn left onto a lane marked with a dead-end sign. The tarmac turns to grassy track and leads you past two abandoned farmhouses, which bear testament to the declining population of this upland area.

Follow the track through two gates to arrive at a tarmac road. Turn left and follow the road uphill beside a tall hedge of hawthorn. As the road reaches its highest point and swings right, turn left onto a bog track. Pass through a gate and follow the track uphill

Route 10

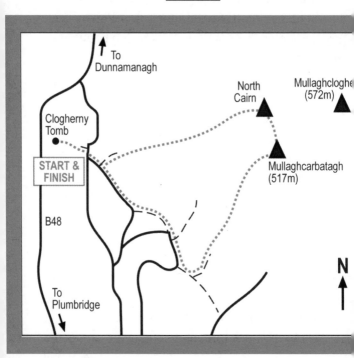

·········· Route Described

for 100m, then turn left again onto a rougher track.

The track soon peters out on spongy ground but you should continue climbing northeast across the close-cropped turf to the broad top of Craigacorm (323m). An old fence can now be seen running along the top of the ridge to the summit of Mullaghcarbatagh.

Follow the western side of the fence, where grazed ground affords relatively easy walking. Descend through a boggy col to the boundary of the Bradkeel forestry plantation, where you will need to cross briefly to the eastern side of the ridge to avoid the plantation.

The gradient increases as the ridge swings away from the forest, and small outcrops of rock begin to appear between the grass and heather. It is not long now before you arrive at the summit cairn, a beehive-shaped construction almost 3m tall. On a clear day the views are tremendous. To the south the Sperrin range falls away to the Glenelly and Owenkillew valleys. To the west and northwest lie the rugged outline of Donegal's Blue Stack Mountains and the unmistakable pyramid of Errigal.

The panorama is blocked only by the broad bulk

of Mullaghclogher to the east. To add an ascent of this peak, simply follow the broad ridge east to the summit cairn, then retrace your steps to Mullaghcarbatagh.

To continue on the circuit, head northwest from Mullaghcarbatagh. Cross a broad and, by local standards, rugged ridge to the prominent cairn and cross at the northwest top of the mountain.

Descend by following a fence southwest across steep, heather-clad slopes, heading towards the edge of Bradkeel forest. Trace the northern boundary of the forest for a few hundred metres, then head southwest across open ground. Aim for the partially ruined gable wall of an old cottage. Here you pick up a green track leading down to the road. Turn right at the road and walk the short distance back to the parking area.

ROUTE 11:
COUNTY DERRY/TYRONE — HILL WALK
SAWEL AND DART MOUNTAINS

A rugged mountain circuit over the highest peak in the Sperrins.

Grade: **4**
Time: **5¹/₂-6¹/₂ hours**
Distance: **14km (8¹/₂ miles)**
Ascent: **650m (2100ft)**
Map: **OSNI 1:50,000 sheet 13.**
Start & Finish: The route starts and finishes from the B47 Plumbridge-Draperstown road around 2km east of Sperrin village (grid reference: H654946). Look for a track on the northern side of the road roughly 200m east of a farm. The bottom of the track is marked by a makeshift gate set at an angle to the road. Either park carefully along the verge beside the track or head west along the B47 and find better parking places between here and the point where the descent route joins the road, 3.5km to the west.

INTRODUCTION

This circuit explores the very heart of the Sperrin Mountains, Northern Ireland's second highest mountain group. The range gets its name from the gaelic *Cnoc Speirín*, meaning 'the pointed hills'. The label is something of a misnomer, however, because there are no airy ridges or plunging cliffs here. But pick a good day for your walk when the ground is dry and the views are at their best, and you'll find there's no better way to appreciate the landscape of Tyrone and Derry than from the top of a Sperrins peak.

This route is the area's classic upland outing. It begins by climbing to the summit of Sawel Mountain, the highest point of the range at 678m. Also on the itinerary is neighbouring Dart Mountain (619m), whose exposed rock outcrops make it the most distinctive peak in the chain.

Tracks ease your progress on the approach and descent routes but rough mountainous terrain must be negotiated between the two summits. A series of fences provide directional guidance across the high ground but navigational skills are still required in bad weather. The route finishes with

3.5km of road walking, which can be avoided if you have two vehicles.

THE ROUTE

Begin by passing through the makeshift gate at the bottom of the track. The track is rather faint at first but it becomes better defined as it curves around into Glenerin. Already Sawel is clearly visible ahead.

After after 1.5km the track descends to a sheep fold beside a stream. Cross the stream, an easy task in normal conditions but difficult after rain. The track consolidates beyond the stream, now providing a firm walking surface.

Continue to follow the track northwest above Binleana Burn, soon passing a ruined cottage and a small forest plantation. On the horizon you may notice the outline of County Rock, a conspicuous boulder that stands on the boundary between Counties Derry and Tyrone. The track climbs close to the rock and joins a tarmac road at Sawel Gap.

Cross the road and begin to climb directly up the steep slope on the other side, following a fence that marks the county boundary. Pass to the right of several rock outcrops and continue to a junction of fences. Cross the fence on the right and continue

Route 11

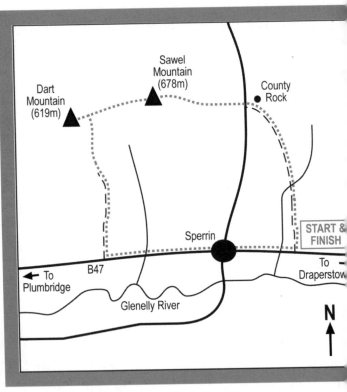

Route Described

climbing, with the ground becoming firmer under-foot as you gain height.

Follow the fence until it veers away to the south. You are now just 150m from the top of Sawel. Head west over open ground to the cairn and trig point that marks the highest point of the rounded summit plateau. The views are worth the climb. The rest of the Sperrins range stretches away to the east and west while the coast of Antrim can be seen to the north.

Cross a stile near the summit and descend southwest across rough bog and peat hags. You lose around 140m in height on your way to the col beneath Dart Mountain. Though Dart is lower in elevation than Sawel, its rocky profile gives it more character. Unusually for this region, some of the schist that forms the foundation of the Sperrins is exposed here as boulders and small rock outcrops.

Halfway across the col between Sawel and Dart you meet another fence, this time running to the top of Dart. Follow the fence southwest, climb-ing through a shallow gully to the summit. A cairn and improvised cross mark the top. In some ways the views from here are even better than from Sawel, with Mullaghclogha and the Glenelly Valley prominent to the west and south.

To descend from the mountain, begin by retracing your steps for around 400m to a rocky knoll. Now bear right along a fence that leads onto the broad spur of Oughtmame. Follow this fence over rough tussock grass to a junction with another fence. It's worth checking behind you as you descend to see the changing perspective of Dart and Sawel.

At the fence junction, turn left and pass through a gate beside a small conifer plantation. Continue to descend and within 200m you join a grassy lane. The lane passes through several more gates and arrives at the B47. Turn left and follow the road for 3.5km back to the start.

ROUTE 12:
COUNTY DERRY/TYRONE — HILL WALK
THE EASTERN SPERRINS

Enjoy fine views on this accessible mountain circuit at the eastern edge of the range.

Grade: 3
Time: 3-4 hours
Distance: 9km (5½ miles)
Ascent: 450m (1480ft)
Maps: OSNI 1:50,000 sheets 13, 7 and 8.
Start & Finish: The circuit starts and finishes beside Glenedra Bridge, at the southern side of Banagher Forest (grid reference: C706003). The bridge is located on the B40 Feeny-Draperstown road, around 10km southeast of Feeny and 9km north-west of Draperstown. Two forest tracks lead south off the road either side of the bridge. Park at the entrance to the easternmost track, where there is space for around six vehicles.

INTRODUCTION
This compact mountain horseshoe explores the

eastern tip of the main Sperrins range. Straddling the border between Counties Derry and Tyrone, the route visits Mullaghaneany (627m), Oughtmore (569m) and Spelhoagh (568m). Mullaghaneany is the Sperrins' third highest peak and its location makes it a fine vantage point for the rounded, whaleback ridges of the rest of the range.

Though geologists claim the Sperrins are founded on schists and quartzites, a heavy covering of peat means there's little evidence of any rock on this circuit. The scarcity of material makes it difficult to build cairns, and none of the summits are marked by the traditional pile of stones normally associated with Irish mountains.

The route benefits from a starting and finishing point at 300m, and the firm surface of a forest track takes much of the strain out of the initial climb. The high ground consists of rough but dry trussock grass. Navigation skills are required in bad weather but in clear conditions, route finding is a relatively straightforward affair. A fence runs across all the summits on the circuit and provides consistent directional guidance.

To extend the route, consider adding an ascent of Meenard Mountain (620m). Head west at the summit of Mullaghaneany and descend along the ridge to a col, then climb to Meenard summit. The 3km detour will add about 180m of an ascent and one hour to your day.

THE ROUTE

From the parking area, join the road and turn left across Glenedra Bridge. On the opposite side of the bridge, turn left beside a ruined stone building onto a track signed for Banagher Forest. Pass a metal gate and follow the gravel track into the trees.

Climb steadily through the conifer plantation to a fork after roughly 1km. Keep right here and continue climbing straight up the hill. In another kilometre you arrive at a second junction, where you should turn left.

Around 300m beyond the last junction you reach a wide fire-break on the right. This is your access route to the mountains. Turn right and climb over tussock grass to the top of the trees. Cross a fence and you are now out onto an open mountain slope northeast of Mullaghaneany.

Climb steadily southwest over rough but relatively dry ground. The angle of ascent soon eases and a fence arrives from the left. Follow the fence

Route 12

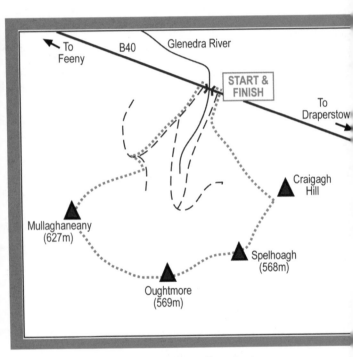

.... Route Described

88

over the broad, rounded plateau. The summit itself is rather indistinct, marked only by a low stone plaque and a junction of three fences.

Fortunately the views compensate for the lack of drama on the ground. The main peaks of the Sperrins stretch away to the east, while in the distance you should be able to make out Donegal's Derryveagh Mountains and the waters of Lough Foyle.

If you want to make the detour to Meenard Mountain, head west along the ridge from Mullaghaneany. To continue on the main circuit, keep the fence on your right and begin to descend southeast. The fence continues around the remaining high ground of the circuit, and the simple instruction is to follow it all the way to Craigagh Hill at the northeastern corner of the horseshoe.

From Mullaghaneany you descend southeast to a col and pass round the top of the forestry plantation. A short, steep ascent then brings you to more gentle slopes and the top of Oughtmore.

Continue along the broad ridge, heading northeast over Spelhoagh towards Craigagh Hill. The occasional peat hag breaks through the tussock grass underfoot. Across the valley to the north a prominent communications mast indicates the top of Mullaghmore.

Continue along the ridge until another fence arrives from the left, just above a shallow gully. The gully marks your descent route off the ridge. Cross the fence and descend to the base of the depression. Now turn left and follow the gully northwest, heading towards a track and small lough at the edge of the forest below.

Where the gully peters out, continue ahead over a series of small undulations. Thick heather underfoot makes this the roughest terrain of the circuit, though fortunately the difficulties are short lived.

Join the track at an open turning area and follow it downhill. Veer right at a fork and continue to descend, now with the nascent Glenedra River to your left. Follow the track downstream for around 800m to return to Glenedra Bridge.

ROUTE 13:
BELFAST — HILL WALK
CAVE HILL

A short but highly rewarding circuit offering fantastic views over Belfast city.

Grade: 2
Time: 2–2½ hours
Distance: 7km (4½ miles)
Ascent: 270m (885ft)
Map: OSNI 1:50,000 sheet 15.
Start & Finish: The route starts and finishes at a car park beneath Belfast Castle (grid reference: J328789). To reach the area, follow signs for Belfast Castle and Cave Hill Country Park from Antrim Road, at the northwest of the city. Pass through the entrance gate and follow the driveway uphill to a fenced parking area on the left shortly before the castle. Belfast city busses also serve the area.

INTRODUCTION
Cape Town has Table Mountain, Edinburgh has Arthur's Seat, and Belfast has Cave Hill. It's one of

those mandatory excursions; no visitor or local should spend long in the city without making the trip to the top. No other vantage point can provide such views over the capital, and the circuit takes just a couple of hours to complete.

The hill is part of Cave Hill Country Park, a 750 acre site at the northwest of the city that includes Belfast Castle and Belfast Zoo. Rising to 368m, the eastern slopes of Cave Hill fall away in a series of sheer escarpments that culminate at the prow of McArt's Fort. Though little can be seen above ground today, this promontory once held a ceremonial ring fort dating back around 3,000 years. The popular name for the prow is Nelson's Nose, a reference to the hill's face-like profile when viewed from the south.

Three waymarked walking trails between 1.5km and 7km in length explore the slopes of Cave Hill from Belfast Castle. This walk is based on the longest route, the green Cave Hill Trail. It follows a mixture of surfaced and unsurfaced paths, and includes several short sections that are steep or rough underfoot. Waymarking is good until you arrive near the top of the hill but thereafter you will need to watch out for turnings. The route passes very close to the top of the cliffs so make sure to take care near the edge.

THE ROUTE

Begin from the information board beside the car park. A low plaque indicates the green Cave Hill Trail uphill along a gravel path. After 100m turn right at a trail junction and head north along the slope into deciduous woodland.

You will pass several more junctions in the trees, each one marked by a trail plaque. Occasional flights of steps punctuate the ascent as the path weaves its way uphill. A steep section of trail then climbs out of the trees to a lookout, where you enjoy the first real views over Belfast Lough. Behind you, the escarpment of Cave Hill looms overhead.

Follow the gravel path to a signed junction beneath the cliffs. The Cave Hill Trail branches left here onto a smaller, earthen footpath known as the Sheep's Path. The gaping mouth of the lowest cave can be seen in the cliff face ahead. The cliff holds no less than five caves, all of which have been chiselled from the basalt rock by humans. It's thought they were used as temporary shelters in times gone by.

<u>Route 13</u>

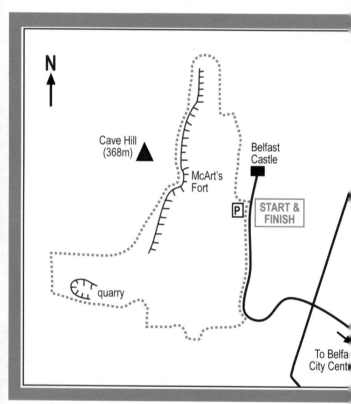

---------- Route Described

94

Follow the narrow trail as it swings to the right beneath the cave and climbs around the top of a hollow known as the Devil's Punchbowl. A steady ascent then leads past another viewpoint to a stile. Pass over the stile and turn left along the northern shoulder of Cave Hill.

Follow the obvious trail uphill over short grass. The prominent mast to the southwest marks the 360m-high summit of Colinward. Cross another stile and continue climbing to the edge of the cliffs.

The prow of McArt's Fort can now be seen jutting out from the cliffs ahead. Follow the cliff line south to the base of the promontory, where a turnstile and flight of steps allow access to the top. Your reward for reaching this point is a fantastic panorama over Northern Ireland's eastern seaboard, with views stretching from the Antrim Hills in the north to the Mourne Mountains in the south. Belfast lies immediately beneath you with the docks and shipyard prominent at the centre of the city.

Retrace you steps off the prow and turn left onto a gravel path. Follow the path south along the cliff line, then pass a stile and swing away from the cliffs. The best views are now over the green, rounded hummocks of the Belfast Hills.

Descend through gorse and hawthorn to another stile. You now need to take care because the next turn is not marked. Continue to another stile on the left of the path. The gravel trail continues ahead but this route turns left across the stile to join a grassy path.

Descend over the grass to the top of an old quarry. Follow the path into a meadow and turn left. Keep to the high ground as you cross the field and pass through a gap in the hedge. The path now descends along the edge of the quarry, a pretty spot that has been reclaimed by nature.

Pass through a turnstile and cross a small stream. A steep, rough section of path now leads back into the woodland. Join a wider gravel path and turn right, continuing your descent through the trees. Turn left at the next fork to arrive at the entrance driveway. Turn left and follow the road uphill for 500m to return to the car park beneath the castle.

ROUTE 14:
COUNTY DOWN – COASTAL WALK
NORTH DOWN COASTAL PATH

A paved footpath passing busy marinas and sandy beaches on the shore of Belfast Lough.

Grade: 2
Time: 4½–5½ hours
Distance: 20km (12½ miles)
Ascent: 60m (200ft)
Map: OSNI 1:50,000 sheet 15.
Start & Finish: The official starting point of the route is the maypole at the junction of Shore Road and High Street in Holywood town centre (grid reference: J398793). Holywood is situated on the A2 Belfast-Bangor road, around 10km east of Belfast city centre. Parking is available in various town-centre car parks.

The route finishes in Groomsport village, around 17km east of Holywood along the A2 (grid reference: J537835). A convenient car park can be found on the eastern side of the harbour.

INTRODUCTION

Beginning just 10km from the heart of Belfast, this route springs from industrial surrounds. First impressions from Holywood seafront can be rather off-putting. Freighters plough the busy shipping lanes of Belfast Lough, aeroplanes pass overhead on the final approach to the harbour airport, and the smokestack of Kilroot power station lies directly across the bay.

Despite its urban beginnings, the path spends a surprising amount of time exploring relatively natural terrain. Rocky headlands, secluded bays and native woodlands are just some of the highlights of the route. The abundant birdlife has become accustomed to walkers and you may be rewarded with close-up views of normally shy species. Keep an eye out too for grey Atlantic seals visiting from their colony on the Copeland islands.

The route generally follows the grassy flats just above the shoreline. The path is surfaced for most of its length and you will need little more than a pair of running shoes on your feet. Despite its linear format, two vehicles are not really necessary. A railway runs from Holywood to Bangor, with frequent onward bus connections from Bangor to Groomsport at the end of the route. Together the services provide a convenient way to return to the start of the walk.

THE ROUTE

From the maypole in Holywood town centre, walk northwest along Shore Road. Cross the A2 and pass under the rail bridge to reach the sea front. The path is now signed northeast along the promenade.

Follow the concrete path between the shore and the railway tracks. In approximately 2km you arrive at *Cultra*, home to the Royal North of Ireland Yacht Club. The name Cultra means 'back of the beach'.

Continue along the path to the Royal Belfast Golf Club at Craigavad, about 2km further on. You will soon begin to appreciate the huge popularity of sailing and golf in this area as there are several more golf courses and yacht clubs to pass.

From Craigavad to Grey Point you'll notice an increasing number of sea birds along the rocky coastal shelves. Oystercatchers and curlews are particularly obvious. The scenery changes again as you enter the woodland of Crawfordsburn Country Park. The next 3.5km are spent along the shore of

Route 14

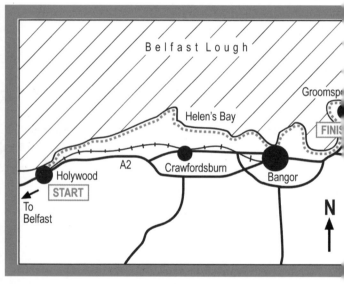

·········· Route Described

this popular country park.

Follow the path through the trees to Grey Point. The headland commands a fine view of Belfast Lough and was an obvious site for the area's war defences. A side path leads to Grey Point Fort, which was built in 1907 and functioned throughout both world wars until its closure in 1957. It had two six-inch artillery guns trained over the water and along with a similar emplacement across the lough at Kilroot, it provided a formidable barrier to unwanted vessels reaching Belfast.

Pass through more broad-leafed woodland to the beach at Helen's Bay, a popular bathing spot. Cross the sand and continue over the small headland that separates Helen's Bay from the wide expanse of Crawfordsburn beach. The buildings of Bangor are now visible ahead.

From Crawfordsburn beach a secluded stretch of path leads around two more small bays, Swineley and Smelt Mill, before turning into Bangor Bay. Bangor was originally a monastic settlement dating from 558 AD and in more recent times it enjoyed prosperity as a Victorian holiday resort. Today the hustle and bustle of the marina comes as something of a shock after the relative isolation of the previous stretch of coastline.

Follow the seafront promenade around Luke's Point to the quieter Ballyholme Bay. The town ends abruptly at the eastern end of this bay. Rejoin the path beside the sea wall and continue towards Ballymacormick Point. The path now leads along the edge of a field into National Trust property. This is another attractive stretch of coastline and seabirds gather once again on the rocky foreshore.

Continue around the headland to the beautiful village of Groomsport. Cockle Island, in the middle of the harbour, is used by breeding pairs of common and Arctic terns after their 10,000 mile journey from the Antarctic. Down by the harbour you will find Cockle Row, two restored seventeenth-century cottages that are the village's main attraction. The bus stop and car park that mark your journey's end are also situated near the harbour.

ROUTE 15:
COUNTY ANTRIM/DOWN — WATERSIDE WALK
LAGAN TOWPATH

A flat, linear route along wooded river banks between two urban centres.

Grade: 1
Time: 3^1/$_2$-4^1/$_2$ hours
Distance: 14.5km (9 miles)
Ascent: 60m (200ft)
Maps: OSNI 1:50,000 sheets 15 and 20.
Start & Finish: The route starts at a car park beside Cutter's Wharf bar, on Lockview Road in the Stranmillis area of Belfast (grid reference: J340713). There is a city bus stop adjacent to the car park and the closest train station is Belfast Botanic.

The official finishing point is the car park for the Lisburn City Council buildings, located at the end of Canal Street in Lisburn (grid reference: J273643). Lisburn Central train station is a short walk from the car park.

INTRODUCTION

The Lagan Valley Regional Park is a surprisingly natural corridor of greenery that springs from the heart of Belfast city. Extending for almost 18km along the banks of the River Lagan, the park links the urban centres of Belfast and Lisburn.

This route follows the towpath along the length of the park. Once the preserve of barge horses, the path has retained its traditional course between the banks of the river and stretches of canal. The dual waterway system was devised in the 1700s as a means of transporting goods to port in Belfast. Barges would navigate the river wherever possible but where the flow was too steep they would divert onto artificial canals. A series of locks would help them negotiate the different water levels before they returned to the river.

A paved footpath is followed throughout, with the exception of a short detour onto a gravel surface in Belvoir Forest Park. Casual sports shoes are more than adequate for your feet. Signposting is good and marker posts count the miles from start to finish.

Despite the linear format, frequent bus and train services mean that return transport is not a problem. Most people catch the train from Lisburn back to Belfast at the end of the walk. The route can be shortened by joining it at various stages along the route, notably at Shaw's Bridge to shave 3.5km off the total distance.

THE ROUTE

From the car park on Lockview Road, follow a tarmac footpath south through the trees. Pass a Lagan Valley information board and join the river beside a weir.

The towpath leads upstream along tree-lined banks that could be a million miles from Belfast. Pass the first bridge and continue to a second wooden bridge, situated just beyond the one-mile marker post. The official towpath continues straight on, but for a pleasant variation turn left and cross the bridge to Belvoir Forest Park.

On the opposite side of the river, turn right and follow a gravel path into the forest. Climb around a bend above the river and turn right at a junction. Now descend through the woodland to a gap in a wall. Turn right here to return to the canal.

Cross a bridge over the canal and rejoin the towpath beside a lock-keeper's cottage. Turn left

<u>Route 15</u>

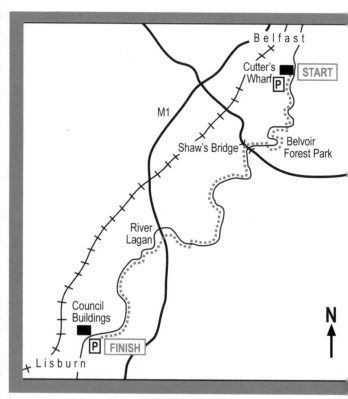

·········· Route Described

and follow the path until it swings across a larger bridge over the main river. You now find yourself at Newforge Lane car park and bus stop, another access point for the towpath.

Turn left and follow signs through the parking area to Clement Wilson Park. Rejoin the footpath and continue across the middle of grassy parkland. Before long you arrive at Shaw's Bridge, a busy traffic thoroughfare. As you pass beneath the bridge you will notice a series of small weirs and slalom posts along the river, marking a popular practice spot for local kayakers.

At Shaw's Bridge car park turn left through a wooden gateway, following a sign for the Ulster Way. Continue along the river to the wooden Gilchrist Bridge and on past some new apartments built on the site of an old water-powered linen mill.

The river branches off at Eel Weir but the towpath continues straight ahead along the wooded banks of the canal. Pass under a road bridge, then cross a metal footbridge to the opposite bank. The noise of traffic now increases as you approach the M1 motorway. Follow the path as it swings away from the water and passes through a pedestrian tunnel beneath the road.

Rejoin the canal and continue for about 1km to another road bridge, a red stone structure that reaches high above the water. The next landmark is an old brick building beside the canal that currently serves as a Coca-Cola bottling factory. You must now cross a minor road and, 1km later, another road.

There are increasing signs of the urban environment until you pass beneath a sculpted metal gateway and suddenly find yourself at the car park beside Lisburn council offices. The five tiers of Union Locks are on your right, marking the official end of the route.

To reach Lisburn train station, cross the lock gate to the island that holds the cream-coloured council buildings. Continue straight ahead over a footbridge to the opposite side of the river. Turn left along the bank and pass a tiered weir to arrive at a major road junction. Cross the dual carriageway and continue uphill along Bridge Street to the market square. The train station is located directly across the square at the end of Railway Street.

ROUTE 16:
COUNTY DOWN — WATERSIDE/WOODLAND WALK
CASTLE WARD

A scenically varied circuit around a National Trust estate on the shore of Strangford Lough.

Grade: 1
Time: 2-3 hours
Distance: 8km (5 miles)
Ascent: 40m (130ft)
Map: OSNI 1:50,000 sheet 21.
Start & Finish: The circuit starts and finishes at the main car park for Castle Ward National Trust estate (grid reference: J573494). The estate is signed off the A25 Downpatrick-Strangford road, around 12km northeast of Downpatrick and 2km south-west of Strangford.

INTRODUCTION
The 25km long sea inlet of Strangford Lough is a haven for wildlife and water sports enthusiasts, yet relatively little of its shoreline is open to walkers.

The National Trust estate of Castle Ward, at the southwestern corner of the lough, offers some of the best waterside trails available.

The 850 acre estate contains six colour-coded walking trails, ranging from 2km to 5km in length. This route combines several trails on a circuit through woodland and along the lough shore. It follows a mixture of surfaced and unsurfaced paths, and waymarking is good throughout. Besides the colour markers of the estate trails, the route also follows a section of the Lecale Way, which has replaced the old Ulster Way in this area. There is a charge for entry to the estate but in return you will receive a trail map that is much more useful than the OS map for walking purposes.

In its relatively short distance the route passes two tower houses, Castle Ward and Audley's Castle, and there are views of other keeps elsewhere along the lough shore. The region is dotted with similar buildings, which date back to the period when Portaferry was a major port. Most were constructed during the fifteenth or sixteenth centuries, spurred on by King Henry VI's offer of £10 to anyone who would erect a tower to protect the coastline.

THE ROUTE

Head uphill to the top of the gravel parking area and follow signs for the adventure playground. The walking trail begins beside the playground at a wooden gate signed for Castle Ward Forest.

Begin by following the green trail markers. Pass through the gate and head along a grass track towards the forest. Climb gently to a T-junction and turn left into the trees. About 50m later, turn right along a narrow footpath to reach a small lough. Join a track at the water's edge and turn right.

Follow the track around the lough and along the edge of several open meadows. Pass a stand of majestic beech trees at the southern boundary of the estate before plunging into a stand of dark pines. A smaller path weaves through the trees to emerge onto a tarmac driveway near the main entrance gate.

The green trail turns left along the driveway but this route crosses the road and continues straight ahead along a track, now following markers for the red trail. The track leads through the trees, descending slightly to reach a small camping ground.

Cross the road beneath the camping ground

Route 16

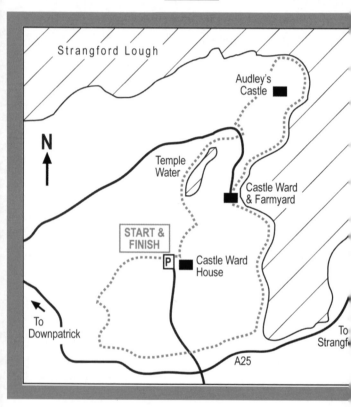

·········· Route Described

and continue straight ahead. You now join a wide avenue and begin to head north along the lough shore. The surrounding woodland allows only an occasional glimpse of the water to your right.

Follow the avenue for roughly 1km to a T-junction with a tarmac lane. Turn right here to reach the Strangford Lough Wildlife Centre, which is well worth a visit. The lane then leads to a courtyard containing a farm and the old tower house of Castle Ward, where the original estate building was built in the 1570s. Turn right at the centre of the courtyard and pass beneath a stone archway to reach the lough shore.

Continue along the shore on a gravel track, now following markers for the blue trail and signs for the Ulster Way. Pass in front of Strangford Sailing Club, where there are great views east across the lough to Portaferry. Join a footpath and continue across a pebble beach to arrive beneath Audley's Castle.

Turn right along a grassy trail and trace the shoreline around the base of the castle. Pass through a metal gate, where there are good views north along the length of the lough. You now head back into woodland and swing left to join the end of a gravel lane just west of the castle. A turnstile allows a quick detour to visit the fifteenth-century tower house itself.

Follow the lane to a minor road and turn left. This brings you to another junction 150m later. Leave the road here and turn right through a stone gateway onto a track. Continue past the pretty lough of Temple Water and swing left onto a tree-lined pathway.

Where the trees end, continue straight ahead along the red route, following signs for the house. Climb a grass bank and pass under a stone bridge, then turn right along a track. After 80m veer left and use a tunnel to reach the back of the main estate house. Either turn left to visit the dual facades of the eighteenth century mansion, or turn right to return to the car park.

ROUTE 17:
COUNTY DOWN — COASTAL WALK
BALLYHORNAN COASTAL PATH

A linear route along one of the wildest stretches of coastline in County Down.

Grade: 2
Time: 2½-3½ hours
Distance: 11km (7 miles)
Ascent: 60m (200ft)
Map: OSNI 1:50,000 sheet 21.
Start & Finish: The route starts at a parking area for Killard Nature Reserve (grid reference: J599441). The lay-by is marked by an information board and is located on the Kilclief-Ballyhornan coastal road, around 1.5km south of Kilclief and 2.5km north of Ballyhornan. The area is accessed via the A2 Strangford-Ardglass road.

The route finishes in the centre of Ardglass. There is plenty of parking space at the marina and elsewhere around the village.

INTRODUCTION

This walk explores the rocky coastline around the village of Ballyhornan. It begins with a trip around Killard Nature Reserve and the entire route falls within the Lecale Area of Outstanding Natural Beauty. On its way along the coast it crosses sandy beaches, rocky foreshore and grassy banks, with 2.5km of tarmac at the end of the route. The section from Ballyhornan to Ardglass forms part of the Lecale Way and is fully waymarked.

As with most coastal walks, the character of this route is determined to a large extent by the state of the sea. In high winds and large swells the sea creates a very different impression to calm, summer conditions. The tide is also important; at low tide it is a simple matter to cross the firm sand of two beaches near the start of the walk. At high tide you' will be restricted to more awkward pebbles and rocks at the top of the beach. For the easiest passage, avoid starting the route around high tide.

Despite the linear format, two vehicles are not strictly necessary. The Ulsterbus Lecale Rambler service will transport you between start and finish on weekends in July and August. At other times, daily Ardglass-Ballyhornan bus services mean you can at least complete the route between those two points.

THE ROUTE

The route begins at an information board for Killard Nature Reserve at the southern end of the parking lay-by. From here, descend a grass bank to the shoreline and turn right. Follow a faint foot-path through the grass or cross the beach to reach a wooden gate after 300m.

Pass through the gate and join a path through grassy meadows. This is Killard Nature Reserve, and the meadows are alive with birds and wild-flowers during the summer. If the tide is retreat-ing the sea to the north is likely to be turbulent, as 400,000 tonnes of tidal water empties out of the narrow mouth of Strangford Lough. Little wonder that the Vikings named the inlet *Strang Fjörthr*, or strong fiord.

Follow the path around the headland, keeping close to the shore to reach a sandy beach at the southern side of the promontory. Cross the beach to the rocks at its western end. You now have to negotiate 400m of awkward ground, hopping over

Route 17

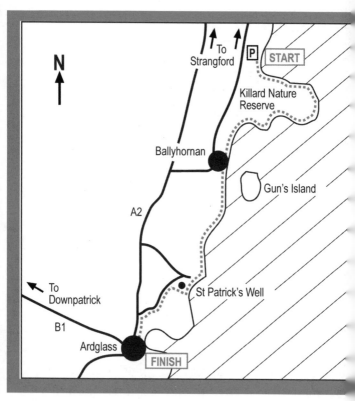

.... Route Described

the boulders along the shore. This is the most difficult terrain of the route and it's a relief to round the outcrop and drop onto the firm sand of Ballyhornan Strand.

Follow the beach to its southern tip, 1km away. Gun's Island, named after a cannon that was washed ashore from a shipwreck, lies 500m out to sea and can be reached on foot at spring low tides. At the end of Ballyhornan Strand, pass through a gateway to a tarmac lane. Turn left and follow the road along the shore. The road soon dwindles to a track, which deposits you at a shingle cove.

Cross the pebbles and join a footpath on the opposite side. The path leads past a ruined coastguard station and around several more small coves. You then cross a concrete stile and climb a bank, beginning to undulate over grassy ground at the back of the shore.

The coastline becomes wilder and more dramatic as you continue, and you are soon forced to the top of the cliffs by a steep inlet. Continue along the slope, with short grass providing an easy walking surface underfoot. The Mourne Mountains are now visible to the southwest and the Isle of Man lies out to sea.

Cross a stile beneath a lone house and continue through longer grass to Sheepland, an abandoned settlement that once held a corn mill. The path now returns to sea level and passes a memorial to a diver killed offshore in 1998. Continue around the coast to the wooden cross and enclosure surrounding St Patrick's Well, a site associated with the saint's arrival in County Down in 432 AD.

Shortly beyond the well, the path arrives at a grass lane. Turn right along the lane and pass between tall hedges to a minor road. Turn left here and follow the tarmac for a little over 1km to a junction, then turn right. In 400m you arrive at the A2 Strangford-Ardglass road. Turn left and follow the tarmac for 1km to arrive at the centre of Ardglass.

ROUTE 18:
COUNTY ARMAGH – WOODLAND WALK
PEATLANDS PARK

Waymarked trails explore a protected enclave of raised bog and native woodland.

Grade: 1
Time: 2-3 hours
Distance: 9km (5¹/₂ miles)
Ascent: 40m (130ft)
Map: OSNI 1:50,000 sheet 19.
Start & Finish: The route starts and finishes at the main car park for Peatlands Country Park (grid reference: H903605). To reach the park follow signs north from junction 13 of the M1 motorway, situated 11km east of Dungannon and 56km west of Belfast.

INTRODUCTION

Within a total area of 650 acres, Peatlands Country Park occupies a flat, low-lying site near the south-western shore of Lough Neagh. Ten thousand years of poor drainage in the area has produced thick bogs, many of which were cut for fuel between the eighteenth and twentieth centuries. Today the mixture of bog and natural woodland is recognised as a rare and valuable natural habitat and is protected within two nature reserves.

The park contains five waymarked trails between 2km and 9km long. The route described follows the red Peatlands Walk, which explores both nature reserves and includes a trip to Derryadd Lake in the far southeastern corner of the park. To add or subtract mileage, it's relatively simple to combine the route with the other trails in the park.

Managed paths are followed throughout, and many sensitive sections of trail are surfaced with wood chip. Running shoes or light walking boots are more than adequate for your feet. Other attractions include a demonstrative turf-cutting operation and a narrow gauge railway, while the visitor centre provides exhibits on the history and natural history of the area.

The park pamphlets and map boards generally show the trails in more detail than the OS map.

THE ROUTE

From the car park, follow signs towards the visitor centre. Before you arrive at the centre you will come to a covered map board. The first sign for the red Peatlands Walk is located beside the board.

Follow the paved footpath to the edge of the car park and turn right. Waymarking arrows lead around a field and across the railway tracks. Turn right here and follow a tree-lined avenue into deciduous woodland.

Turn left onto a gravel path at the next junction. Pass a pond and head out towards the edge of the 22-hectare Mullenakill Nature Reserve. The route now veers north along the eastern edge of the reserve, using alternate stretches of duckboard and wood chip to cope with the soft and delicate ground.

Mullenakill protects the largest area of uncut raised bog in Counties Armagh and Down. Though this particular ground has never been dug, it has suffered from the drainage of adjoining bogland. A completely natural raised bog is thickest and wettest in the centre but the change in drainage patterns has caused the central dome of

Route 18

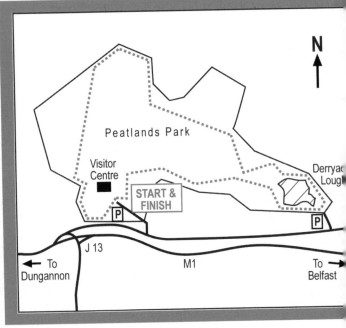

.... Route Described

124

Mullenakill to collapse. Fortunately the fauna and flora of the area remain largely intact.

Continue through a short stretch of woodland and cross more bog on the northwest fringe of the park. A few hundred metres later the trail swings south across Derryhubbert Bog Stream and enters Annagarriff National Nature Reserve.

This reserve contains a swathe of semi-natural deciduous woodland. The woods survived as a hunting reserve for two centuries and, despite felling they have been allowed to regenerate naturally. Oak and birch are dominant species. Annagarriff is also the only place in Ireland you will find the wood ant, whose nests are built to the size of a double bed. Permission to leave the paths in the nature reserve must be sought from the warden.

Follow a hard track through Annagarriff, winding southeast through the trees to a long lane lined with rhododendron. A right turn then leads to Derryane Bog, where the remnants of turf cuttings can be seen. It takes centuries for bog to regenerate and it will be some time before the cuttings in this area are erased.

At the next junction you could take a short cut

by continuing straight ahead over a wooden bridge and following the yellow route back to the car park. To continue on the longer route, turn left towards Derryadd Lake.

Follow the red path across a tarmac lane and turn left at the next junction. A raised turf walkway leads across more cut bog to the lake. Sections of wooden boardwalk then take you on a full circuit of the lake, passing through reed beds growing well over head height.

Follow the path back towards the woodland, turning left across a wooden bridge and re-crossing the road on the way. The trail then turns left and winds through patches of bog and woodland near the southern boundary of the park.

Cross the tracks of the narrow gauge railway and enter a small wood. You emerge from the trees at the turbary site where turf-cutting demonstrations are held in the summer. From here follow a drainage channel south and then west to the car park.

ROUTE 19:
COUNTY FERMANAGH – HILL/WOODLAND WALK
CLIFFS OF MAGHO

A tough ascent is rewarded by spectacular views and a choice of two forest circuits.

Grade: 2
Time: 2-2½ hours
Distance: 5km (3 miles)
Ascent: 300m (985ft)
Maps: OSNI 1:50,000 sheet 17 or OSNI 1:25,000 Fermanagh Lakeland Lower Lough Erne.
Start & Finish: The route starts and finishes at a parking area at the base of the Magho Cliffs (grid reference: H062583). The car park is situated along the A46 Belleek-Enniskillen road, around 13km east of Belleek. A sign for Lough Navar Forest marks the turn.

INTRODUCTION
The Cliffs of Magho dominate the southwestern shores of Lower Lough Erne in County Fermanagh.

The 120m high vertical escarpment rises just 1km from the shore and provides superb views over the watery expanse below.

The trough that holds Lower Lough Erne was gouged by a massive glacier, contained on one side by these ice-scoured cliffs. Today the slopes beneath the quartzite scarp support a semi-natural woodland, which boasts the highest number of woodland species of any site in Northern Ireland. Little wonder that the whole cliff area is protected as an Area of Special Scientific Interest.

This route begins at the bottom of the cliffs. A steep, sustained ascent brings you through the woodland to the top of the precipice. The cliffs are backed by Lough Navar Forest, a 2,600 hectare pine plantation owned by the forestry service. A short inland loop takes you past a lake into the trees, while a longer forest circuit is also described for people who want to extend the walk.

The route spends most of its time on footpaths, though a short section at the top of the cliffs follows the tarmac of the Forest Drive. Some sections of path are rough and wet so boots are recommended.

THE ROUTE

Follow a gravel track uphill from the parking area. When the track ends after 200m, continue along the obvious footpath into the woodland.

The path climbs steadily from the outset and if anything it becomes steeper as you progress. A series of switchbacks and 370-odd steps ease your passage over the steepest sections but the trail is well used and can be muddy when wet. The wooded slope is carpeted with lush vegetation, the vibrant greens of mosses and ferns punctuated by splashes of colour from wildflowers.

It comes as quite a shock to exit the trees at the top of the slope and catch your first glimpse of the view from your new location. Lower Lough Erne is spread out in all its splendour below. You should also be able to pick out the distant silhouettes of Donegal's Bluestack Mountains and Slieve League to the northwest.

Continue along the path to the bottom of a flight of steps. The steps lead up to a car park on the Lough Navar Forest Driveway. You will return through this parking area at the end of the forest loop.

For now, turn right at the base of the steps and

Route 19

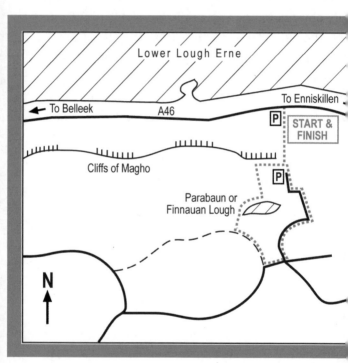

·········· Route Described

follow a gravel path west, passing between the forest and the cliff edge. In about 500m you arrive at a viewpoint where wooden railings protect admirers from the drop below. The sheer rock walls of the cliffs can now be seen to the west.

The lookout marks the end of the surfaced path. Turn south and head over the rough heather directly away from the railings. This is the route of the former Ulster Way and wooden posts topped with yellow arrows mark the route.

Trace the edge of the forestry plantation to a fire-break in the trees, negotiating several patches of wet ground along the way. Now head along the fire-break to reach Parabaun or Finnauan Lough. Turn right at the water's edge and pass around the western tip of the lough. The path enters the trees briefly before turning right again and continuing along another, narrower fire-break to a gravel track.

Here you have a choice of routes. To extend the route and add a 4.5km loop through the forest, turn right and follow the track for 2km to a junction with a tarmac driveway. Turn left here, then left again 800m later. Follow this forest road for another 2km, then turn left to reach the cliff-top car park.

To complete the shorter route, turn left onto the gravel track at the end of the cross-country section. After 300m turn left onto a tarmac road, then left again at a road junction 100m later. This road brings you to the parking area at the top of the cliffs after 1km.

Descend the steps at the cliff side of the car park and rejoin the top of the woodland path. Turn right here and retrace your outward route down the slope to the car park at the base of the cliffs.

ROUTE 20:
COUNTY FERMANAGH —
WATERSIDE/WOODLAND WALK
CASTLE ARCHDALE

A variety of easy trails lead along the shore of Lower Lough Erne in this pleasant country park.

Grade: 1
Time: 2¹/₂-3¹/₂ hours
Distance: 10km (6 miles)
Ascent: 60m (200ft)
Maps: OSNI 1:50,000 sheet 17 or OSNI 1:25,000 Fermanagh Lakeland Lower Lough Erne.
Start & Finish: The route starts and finishes at the Courtyard car park at the heart of Castle Archdale Country Park (grid reference: H176588). The park is situated on the B82 Enniskillen-Kesh road, around 11km north of Enniskillen, and is well signed from the road. Once you arrive in the park follow signs for the Courtyard Centre.

INTRODUCTION
Despite the fact that Lower Lough Erne covers an

area of more than 100km², opportunities for walking along its shores are somewhat restricted Fortunately Castle Archdale offers a good selection of short walking trails. All routes are fully signed and follow a series of tracks and pathways. We describe two circuits, one in the country park (4km) and one in the forest to the north (6km). The loops can be linked together to form a figure-of-eight route of 10km.

The country park occupies an estate formerly owned by the Archdale family. The Courtyard is the only building remaining from a grand manor house built in 1773, and it currently holds the park offices, tea rooms and visitor centre. The old castle from which the estate derives its name is situated in the adjacent forest park. The estate played a key role in history when it became the most westerly British flying boat station during the Second World War. The war years are explained in more detail in a fascinating exhibition at the Courtyard Centre.

Another recommended side trip is to combine the walk with a visit to White Island. White Island once held one of several monastic sites established on Lower Lough Erne. Today visitors can view the ruins of a twelfth-century church and a line of eight stone figures dating from the sixth century. The ferry leaves from Castle Archdale marina, near the Courtyard Centre. Services operate on weekends from Easter to June and daily during July and August.

Before you start your walk it is worth picking up a free park map from the Courtyard visitor centre, which shows the trails in more detail than the OS map.

The Route
The Southern Loop

This loop is marked throughout by yellow arrows on wooden posts. From the Courtyard car park, walk uphill and pass in front of the Courtyard Centre. Follow the gravel path into the trees and turn left. Descend past mixed deciduous woodland and the formal gardens to a junction with a paved path.

Turn right and follow the tarmac past the wild-fowl ponds, butterfly garden and deer enclosure. Continue past the playing fields and through a small car park to reach the shore of Lough Erne.

A very pleasant section of gravel path then leads through the trees at the edge of the water. You will then pass three old stone jetties and as you round a headland, several of the lough's

<u>Route 20</u>

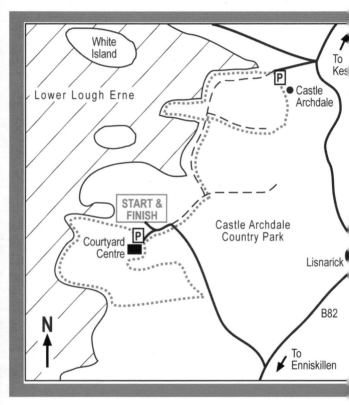

.... Route Described

islands come into view. Turn left and follow a wider gravel trail for a short distance, then turn left again back to the shoreline.

The waterside path brings you to the tip of another promontory, marked by the white cone of The Beacon. A plaque beside the lighthouse commemorates the men killed in one of numerous aeroplane crashes around Lough Erne during the Second World War.

Continue past the Beacon towards Castle Archdale marina. Unless you're planning to catch the ferry to White Island, veer right into the trees shortly before the docks. A short ascent up the steps of the Woodland Walk brings you back to the Courtyard car park.

The Northern Loop

From the car park, follow the main access road away from the Courtyard Centre. Within 200m the road turns right and a gated track continues ahead, signed for 'Castle Archdale Forest'. Pass around the gate and follow this track into the forest.

In approximately 400m you come to a junction; turn left along the trail signed for the castle. The track passes through mixed woodland before arriving at an old cottage and a staggered junction. Here you meet the red waymarking posts that indicate the 3km 'Tom's Island Trail'. Continue past the cottage and turn right towards the castle, as indicated by the second marker post. You will return along the left-hand trail at the end of the loop.

Follow the path though the trees and keep left at a fork. Within 1km you arrive at the ruins of Castle Archdale. Built in the early 1600s, the castle was the original building constructed on the estate when the Archdale family arrived during the plantation of Ulster.

Cross the car park beneath the castle and continue into pine forest. Join the banks of the Hollow River and follow the watercourse to its confluence with Lough Erne. You then trace the lough shore past a jetty to a small gravel beach. White Island lies just offshore and the ruins of the church are clearly visible.

Continue to follow the path around the edge of the promontory known as Tom's Island. The section ends at the junction in front of the old cottage you passed earlier. Turn right and retrace your steps back to the Courtyard car park, following signs to the country park.

ROUTE 21:
COUNTY FERMANAGH –
HILL/WOODLAND WALK
MARBLE ARCH & FLORENCE COURT

A wooded gorge, karst cave systems and a National Trust estate are linked by this waymarked linear route.

Grade: 2
Time: 3-4 hours
Distance: 11km (7 miles)
Ascent: 280m (920ft)
Map: OSNI 1:50,000 sheet 26.
Start & Finish: The route starts at the parking area for Cladagh Gorge (grid reference: H127357). To reach the area, follow signs for Marble Arch Caves from Blacklion, on the A4/N16. Where the caves are signed to the right along the Marlbank Loop road, keep straight ahead. The car park is situated beside Cladagh Bridge 3km further on.

The route finishes at the parking area for Florence Court House (Grid Reference: H175345). Florence Court can be reached by continuing 5km east along the road from Cladagh Gorge. The estate is also well signed from the A4/N16 Eniskillen-Blacklion road.

INTRODUCTION

This walk explores a beautiful section of the Cuilcagh Way in County Fermanagh, linking two of the area's biggest tourist attractions – the Marble Arch Caves and Florence Court House.

The route splits its time between a national nature reserve, a European Geopark and a National Trust estate. The first section of the walk follows a beautiful wooded stream through Cladagh Gorge to Marble Arch Caves. The cave system was first explored in 1897 by E.A. Martel, who used a collapsible boat to cross the underground lake. Today the caverns are ranked among the best show caves in Europe and it is well worth breaking your walk to take a guided tour from the visitor centre.

The middle section of the route winds through fascinating karst landscape that contains some of Ireland's best sinkholes and limestone pavement outside the Burren. The day ends with an exploration of the house and formal gardens at Florence Court.

The route is waymarked throughout and follows

a mixture of footpaths and tarmac lanes. Some sections of path can be rather wet so boots are recommended. The walk is described in a linear format but it can be made into a loop by returning to Cladagh Gorge along the main road between Florence Court and Blacklion. Allow 1½ hours extra for this 5.5km tarmac section and make sure to watch for traffic along the road.

The remainder of this two-day waymarked way climbs Cuilcagh Mountain and is described in route 22 of this guide.

THE ROUTE

From the car park, follow the wide path into Cladagh Gorge. After 500m you pass a small cascade on the left. This waterfall emerges from a spring after an underground journey from a swallow hole called the Rattling Hole higher up on the mountain.

Continue through mature ash woodland until the walls of the gorge close in. Steps then lead up and across Marble Arch, a natural limestone bridge that is the eroded remains of a cave. The Cladagh River now drops underground into the Marble Arch cave system. The path winds up past a huge chasm

Route 21

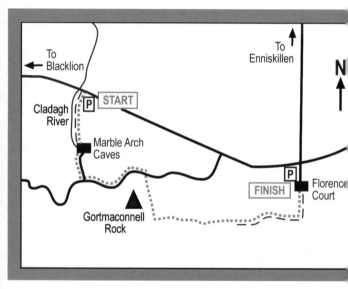

.... Route Described

on the left, and emerges through a gate to the back of Marble Arch visitor centre.

Walk around the right of the visitor centre. Unless you plan to tour the caves, continue through the car park and up the access road. Turn left at the junction with a tarmac lane (the Marlbank Loop road). Follow the tarmac for 1.5km to a stile on the right, flanked by a partly hidden marker post.

Cross the stile onto open ground and head across a rough field at the foot of Gortmaconnell Rock. Cross another small stile and climb onto boggy ground, where views of Cuilcagh open up across a vast expanse of moor to the south. You will notice several abrupt changes in this area from firm, grassy terrain to wet bogland. The firm stretches are underlaid by limestone and the wetter areas by poorly draining sandstone.

Cross another stile and pass some gorse bushes, then look carefully for a waymarking post in the bottom right corner of the field. Cross some wet ground and skirt the edge of a beautifully wooded sinkhole towards another stile. A kilometre of flat, boggy ground then leads to another large sinkhole near a stile.

Cross the stile and follow firm ground to the right of a prominent limestone knoll. Scramble easily onto the flat summit to savour wide-ranging views of Counties Fermanagh, Tyrone and Leitrim.

Descend gently off the eastern side of the knoll and cross a large stile. You now join a farm track and follow it into a lovely wooded valley. Pass a farm and cross a stream to arrive at a junction of tracks. The junction may be unmarked but you should turn left and descend into Florence Court Forest Park.

Keep to the main track through two junctions, then turn right at a third junction. You should now follow the red waymarking posts around the back of the estate. A lovely section of path leads along the edge of a meadow to the impressive formal gardens. It is thought that all yews in Ireland are descended from one tree in this garden.

Continue around to the front of the eighteenth-century Florence Court House. Follow signs from the house to the car park, situated just north-west of the main building.

ROUTE 22:
COUNTY FERMANAGH — HILL WALK
CUILCAGH MOUNTAIN

Two waymarked trails cross a sea of bog and converge at the highest point in County Fermanagh.

Grade: 4
Time: 6-7 hours
Distance: 16km (10 miles)
Ascent: 540m (1770ft)
Map: OSNI 1:50,000 sheet 26.
Start & Finish: The route starts at the car park for Cuilcagh Mountain Park (grid reference: H121335). To reach the area, follow signs for Marble Arch Caves from the A4/N16 Enniskillen-Blacklion road. The car park is located 300m west of the entrance to Marble Arch.

The route finishes at the parking area for Florence Court House (grid reference: H175345). Florence Court is also well signed from the A4/N16 Enniskillen-Blacklion road.

INTRODUCTION

Cuilcagh Mountain (665m) straddles the border of Counties Fermanagh and Cavan. A long, flat-topped peak flanked by a band of steep cliffs, it forms an isolated island in a sea of bog.

The northern slopes of the mountain have been designated as a European Geopark. Much of the low ground around Cuilcagh consists of eroded limestone and shale, while the mountain itself is hard gritstone that is much more resistant to the elements. Despite its composition, the name Cuilcagh has been attributed to the gaelic *Cailceach*, meaning 'chalky'. The label is something of a misnomer because chalk is one substance that does not exist on the mountain.

This route follows two marked walking paths over Cuilcagh, using the Legnabrocky Trail on the approach and the Hiker's Trail on the descent. Of the two routes, the Legnabrocky Trail is far easier because it uses a gravel track to reach the mountain. The Hiker's Trail is unsurfaced and spends much of its time crossing wet blanket bog. If you have an aversion to lengthy bog-trots, you may prefer an out-and-back ascent via the Legnabrocky Trail.

The entire route is marked with frequent, yellow-topped posts, and forms part of the Cuilcagh Way. The remainder of this two-day waymarked way extends from Marble Arch to Florence Court and is described in route 21 of this guide.

THE ROUTE

Cross a stile beside a wooden gate in the southwestern corner of the car park. To the right of the stile is Monastir Sink, a collapsed underground river that links to the Marble Arch Caves.

Follow the gravel track south through limestone meadows, crossing a stone bridge and several more stiles in the early stages. The landscape soon changes to blanket bog but the track continues on, undulating towards Cuilcagh for some 4km. When the gravel comes to an end, a well-marked path continues ahead. Dip across a stream and continue climbing towards the flat-topped escarpment.

The terrain now consists of a mixture of tussock grass and wet moss. Pick your way east of Lough Atona before beginning the final climb to the top. The ground consolidates for the ascent and a muddy trail cuts directly up the steep slope.

Once you reach the summit plateau you have a

<u>Route 22</u>

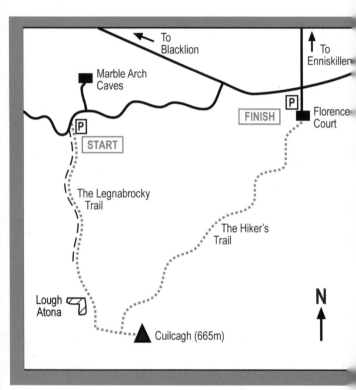

·········· Route Described

choice of routes. The most impressive cliffs are situated to the west, above Lough Atona, and it's well worth making the 1km detour to visit these. To continue directly to the summit, turn left and head east instead.

Cross the heather and stone plateau, passing a small pool and crossing a fence on your way to the trig point at the mountain's eastern edge. The large summit cairn is in fact a Neolithic burial chamber. The views encompass much of Counties Fermanagh, Cavan and Leitrim, and on a very clear day the Irish Sea and the Atlantic Ocean can both be seen in the distance.

Steep cliffs lie immediately north of the summit and the easiest descent route can be found further west. Follow a path along the northern edge of the plateau for about 400m and turn right to start the descent. Cross a stile over a fence, then veer left and follow another fence down the steep slope.

At the bottom of the slope, turn northeast and cross to the eastern side of Altscraghy Gully. The waymarking posts now lead northeast, heading between the hills of Trien and Benaughlin in the distance. You have almost 5km of undulating bog to cross, and the ground is consistently wet underfoot. The challenge is to remind yourself that blanket bog is a rare and precious habitat, despite its inconveniences as a walking surface.

The landscape begins to change as you approach Benaughlin. Farm buildings can be seen to the right as you cross from moorland to grassy meadows. Follow the posts to the edge of Florence Court Forest and cross a wooden stile marked for the Hiker's Trail.

The path now descends along the edge of the forest to a vehicle track. Turn left and keep straight ahead at the following fork, arriving at a T-junction of tracks after approximately 1.5km. Turn left at the T-junction, then take the following two right turns. Shortly after the last turn, head left into the trees along another track. The track dwindles to a footpath and weaves to the right, under a stone archway, to reach the ornamental gardens of Florence Court House.

Turn left and follow a gravel walkway through the garden to the front of the eighteenth-century manor house. The car park that marks the end of the route is situated northwest of the main building and is signed from the house itself.

CO ARMAGH — HILL/WOODLAND WALK
SLIEVE GULLION

This varied circuit on footpaths and lanes includes a
traverse of Armagh's highest mountain.

Grade: 3
Time: 4-5 hours
Distance: 12.5km (8 miles)
Ascent: 500m (1640ft)
Map: OSNI 1:50,000 sheet 29.
Start & Finish: The circuit starts and finishes at the
car park beside the Slieve Gullion Courtyard Centre
in Slieve Gullion Forest Park (grid reference:
J042196). From Newry, take the Dublin road to the
southern edge of town and turn right onto the
B113, signed to Meigh. Continue for about 5km
and turn right at a junction signed for the
Courtyard Centre. Motorists are advised not to
leave valuables in their cars.

INTRODUCTION
Slieve Gullion, the highest mountain in Armagh at
573m, is the centre point of an extinct volcano.

When a massive explosion ripped the mountain apart some 60 million years ago, it left a circle of hills around the main peak. This phenomenon is known by geologists as a ring dyke, and Slieve Gullion provides the finest example of its type in Britain and Ireland.

The mountain is also celebrated by archaeologists. The neolithic burial chamber that marks Slieve Gullion's southern summit is the highest remaining passage tomb in Ireland. The mountain's northern summit also holds a smaller cairn dating from the Bronze Age, around 1800 BC.

For walkers, Slieve Gullion is the focal point of the 57.5km Ring of Gullion waymarked way, which takes two or three days to complete. The one-day circuit described here includes the best section of that longer route. It follows a mixture of forest driveway, narrow country roads and mountain footpath across Slieve Gullion itself. Waymarking posts aid navigation in most places.

If you have two vehicles you could also park at either end of the mountain traverse, leaving a highly enjoyable off-road route of 4km.

THE ROUTE

Begin by following a gravel path uphill from the top left of the car park. The path winds through pleasant deciduous woodland for about 1km before arriving at a log bench on the right. A way-marking post opposite the bench indicates the Ring of Gullion Way.

Cut left over the bank in front of the bench and turn right onto the forest drive. Follow the road uphill, passing through stands of mature beech trees. In 800m you come to a short gravel link track on the right – turn up this and you will arrive at the upper road of the driveway.

Turn left and follow the tarmac around the southern slopes of Slieve Gullion. The open terrain allows expansive views over the ring dyke to the south and east. Keep straight ahead along the road until you reach a car park on the left. This parking area can also be used as a direct starting point for an ascent of Slieve Gullion.

Fifty metres beyond the parking area the mountain path leads off to the right. Though faint at first, it soon consolidates into a well-trodden trail marked by wooden posts. Follow the path

Route 23

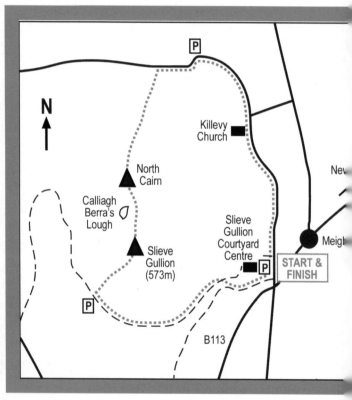

··········· Route Described

uphill to a fence, which is crossed with the aid of a wooden stile, and continue to climb to a stone shelter. Short grass makes for easy progress and the views increase in scope as you gain height.

As you pass the stone shelter the terrain becomes steeper underfoot. The climb is short-lived, however, and it is not long before you arrive at the neolithic tomb that marks the summit of the mountain. It is possible to enter the inner burial chamber by ducking beneath a stone lintel to the right of the approach path. The summit cairn and trig point sit atop the mound of boulders, with 360° views taking in the Mourne Mountains and Carlingford Lough to the east.

Head northwest from the summit, crossing Slieve Gullion's narrow plateau. In about 800m you arrive at Calliagh Berra's Lough. The pool is named after a woman famed in local folklore for bewitch-ing the giant Finn MacCumhaill.

Continue past the lough to the sprawling cairn at the northern summit. The descent path now heads down to the north. Occasional metal arrows mark the way and one or two wet patches of ground need to be crossed.

At a grassy hollow, turn right and join a green

track. The track leads through the heather to a metal gate. Pass through this and veer right across a field to a second gate, which opens onto a road. The gatepost is marked with a painted arrow and indicates an alternative access point for the mountain.

Turn right onto the lane and follow the tarmac as it undulates and then descends through pleasant countryside. Keep right at a fork, where you rejoin the official route of the Ring of Gullion Way. About 1km beyond the junction you pass Killevy Old Church, built on the site of a fifth-century convent. St Bline's holy well is situated at the top of a narrow boreen on the right of the church; the side trip to visit it will add 1km to the walk.

Continue along the road for a further 2.5km and turn right through the gateposts towards the Courtyard Centre. A short climb brings you back to the parking area where you began the circuit.

ROUTE 24:
COUNTY DOWN — WOODLAND WALK
TOLLYMORE FOREST PARK

This varied 'combination trail' makes the most of the scenery in Ireland's oldest forest park.

Grade: 2
Time: 3-4 hours
Distance: 10km (6 miles)
Ascent: 370m (1210ft)
Maps: OSNI 1:50,000 sheet 29, or OSNI 1:25,000 Mourne Country Outdoor Pursuits Map.
Start & Finish: The circuit starts and finishes at the main parking area for Tollymore Forest Park (grid reference: J344325). From the centre of Newcastle, follow signs west towards Bryansford and Tollymore. Turn left off the Bryansford road after 2.5km and pass beneath the ornate Barbican Gate into the park. The main parking area is 1km further on at the end of the Cedar Avenue.

INTRODUCTION
When Tollymore Forest Park was established in

1955 it became the first such park in Britain or Ireland. The 630 hectare reserve includes the formal lakes and gardens of a managed estate, as well as mixed woodland, a large forestry plantation and the tumbling rapids of the Shimna River. All this is set against a backdrop of the Mourne Mountains.

Tollymore has four waymarked walking trails between 2km and 13km long. For first-time visitors the best option is to mix and match the official paths, combining the most interesting features of each route. We suggest a 10km circuit (with a shorter 7km variation) that makes the most of the park's scenery and historic sites. Tracks and footpaths are followed throughout but you will need to keep an eye out for the various turnings. To see the area in better detail it is worth investing in the OS 1:25,000 map.

The park is open every day from 10am to sunset. Entrance costs £4 per car or £2 for adult pedestrians.

THE ROUTE

The route starts at the information board at the southwestern corner of the main car park. For the first 2km you will be following the blue arrows of the Rivers Trail.

Follow the paved footpath away from the information board. After 30m, turn left and pass beneath a stone archway. A formal path known as the Azalea Walk now descends along a stream and brings you to the banks of the Shimna River. Turn right alongside the river and follow a gravel path upstream into mature beech woodland.

Within 500m a side path on the left leads to the Hermitage – a stone, beehive-shaped structure perched above the river. The building was constructed in 1770 as a memorial sanctuary and it remains an atmospheric place. Climb a small flight of stone steps at the back of the structure to return to the main path.

Continue west along the river bank, passing two sets of stepping stones that date back over 200 years. Beyond the confluence of the Shimna and the Spinkwee the beech wood merges into a darker canopy of pines. Follow the river upstream through a lengthy series of rapids to a third set of stepping stones.

The next landmark is the large stone structure of Parnell's Bridge. The blue Rivers Trail turns left here and crosses the bridge but this route continues straight ahead, now following the red arrows

Route 24

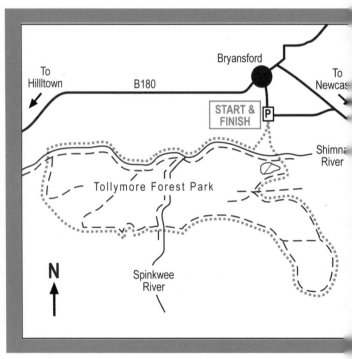

·········· Route Described

of the Long Haul Trail.

Continue along the river bank for a further 500m and cross the wooden Boundary Bridge at the western extremity of the park. You now come to a junction of vehicle tracks. Take the second track on the right, as indicated by a post with a red walker symbol. This is the sign for the Ulster Way, the route you will be following for the next 2km.

Follow the track uphill for 500m and turn right at another junction. This track soon dwindles to an earthen footpath and veers left to climb through the trees. You are now walking along the stone wall that marks the southern boundary of Tollymore, and there are fine views south to the Mourne Mountains.

Rejoin a vehicle track near the top of the rise and continue ahead into dense pines. Descend through a series of switchbacks to a junction above the Spinkwee River.

At this point you have a choice of routes. To return to the car park and save yourself 3km and 100m of ascent, keep straight ahead towards the 'Cascade'. Pass the 10m-high Cascade falls and turn right onto a track that crosses Altavaddy Bridge. Follow the track to the lake, where blue arrows direct you over Old Bridge to the parking area.

To continue on the longer route, turn right at the junction above the Spinkwee and descend across Hore's Bridge. Turn right at the next junction and keep straight ahead at a third, following signs for 'Drinn's View'. The viewpoint itself comes after 1km of steady ascent, where a gap in the trees allows a clear view north over the countryside of County Down.

Continue climbing to a junction and turn right, then keep left at two subsequent junctions. It is not long before the track begins to descend and sweeps round to the left, allowing good views south to Slieve Commedagh. Keep left and then right at the following two junctions, descending through the forest to a small cabin.

Turn right just before the cabin and then left after 250m, now following signs to the 'Lake'. At this point you join the yellow Lakes and Ponds Trail. Veer left to the eastern shore of the lake and continue straight ahead, crossing a grassy bank to the Shimna River. Cross Old Bridge and climb straight up the grassy slope known as the Green Rig to return to the parking area.

ROUTE 25:
COUNTY DOWN – HILL WALK
SLIEVE MEELMORE AND SLIEVE MEELBEG

A neat circuit in the northwestern corner of the Mournes that visits two conical summits.

Grade: 4

Time: 4–5 hours

Distance: 11km (7 miles)

Ascent: 685m (2250ft)

Maps: OSNI 1:50,000 sheet 29, or OSNI 1:25,000 Mourne Country Outdoor Pursuits Map.

Start & Finish: The circuit starts and finishes at the Trassey Track car park, around 9km west of Newcastle (grid reference: J312314). From Newcastle town centre, head west towards Bryansford. Turn left in Bryansford and join the B180 to Hilltown. Four kilometres later, turn left onto a minor road. The Trassey Track car park is situated on the left around 1.5km along this road.

INTRODUCTION
Slieve Meelmore and Slieve Meelbeg translate as

big bald mountain and little bald mountain respectively. The size labels must refer to bulk rather than height, however, because Slieve Meelbeg (708m) is actually the higher of the two summits by 24m.

Besides providing a compact walking circuit, these two mountains also offer superlative vantage points. Summit views sweep across the entire Mourne range, encompassing almost all the area's clustered peaks as well as its intervening loughs and reservoirs.

The route largely follows tracks and well-trodden mountain paths, and includes a return section along the former Ulster Way. This, combined with the presence of the Mourne Wall over the high ground, means that route finding is a relatively simple matter. If you want to extend the circuit, begin by following the Trassey Track to Hare's Gap and add an ascent of Slieve Bearnagh.

THE ROUTE

From the entrance to the car park, turn left and follow the road for 100m. A gravel track now leads off to the left, with an information board signing the Trassey Track. Pass over the stile to the left of the entrance gate and begin to follow the track south.

Two further gates with adjacent stiles are passed before you reach the open terrain of the Mournes. At the final gate, a stone wall can be seen extending west around the base of Slieve Meelmore. The wall marks the line of the old Ulster Way and your return route.

Continue south along the Trassey Track. Wind through a couple of gentle switchbacks before straightening up for the ascent to Hare's Gap, at the southeastern head of the valley. Unless you want to add the ascent of Slieve Bearnagh to the route, however, you will be climbing out of the valley via the col to the southwest.

Follow the Trassey Track for 1.5km to a junction beneath the northern slopes of Slieve Bearnagh. Turn right here and follow a subsidiary track past a small quarry. Where the vehicle track ends, a narrow footpath continues ahead, climbing along the banks of a mountain stream.

As you gain height, the unmistakable line of the Mourne Wall appears at the top of the gap. The final section of path has been constructed with granite slabs, providing an easier walking surface underfoot.

Once at the col, cross the large wooden stile

Route 25

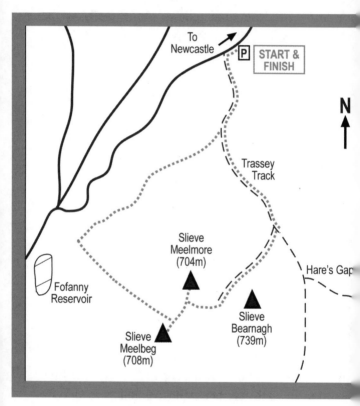

.... Route Described

that spans the wall and turn right. Two walls make their way up Slieve Meelmore from this point: a new wall on the right and an older wall (semi-ruined at the bottom) on the left. The easiest line of ascent can be found beside the old wall.

Climb steeply to the top of the wall and turn right. Now trace another short section of wall to the conspicuous stone shelter, built in 1921, that adorns the summit of Slieve Meelmore. A wooden stile allows you to cross the wall and appreciate the view in all directions. On a clear day Cave Hill marks the location of Belfast to the north, while Lambay Island, northeast of Dublin, can be seen beyond the Silent Valley Reservoir to the south.

Retrace your steps south from the summit, keeping the wall to your right. Descend through a col and then make the 100m climb to Slieve Meelbeg. Though this summit is marginally higher than Slieve Meelmore, it is far less distinctive, marked only by a slight bend in the wall and a small cairn. The new vantage point allows Spelga dam and reservoir to come into view to the west.

From Slieve Meelbeg, return northeast along the wall to the col beneath Slieve Meelmore. Now cross a wooden stile over the wall and begin to descend northwest down the centre of the valley beyond.

Head down the left bank of a stream, with the grassy terrain merging into a stone track towards the bottom of the slope. Follow the track to a junction with the former Ulster Way. Turn right along the footpath, cross the stream and pick up the line of a boundary wall. Follow the path along the wall for almost 2km, passing around the northwestern base of Slieve Meelmore.

Several small streams are crossed before the path brings you back to the Trassey Track. Turn left onto the track and retrace your initial steps back to the car park.

ROUTE 26:
COUNTY DOWN – HILL WALK
SLIEVE COMMEDAGH

An accessible mountain circuit over the second highest peak in Northern Ireland.

Grade: 4
Time: 4-5 hours
Distance: 10km (6 miles)
Ascent: 780m (2560ft)
Maps: OSNI 1:50,000 sheet 29, or OSNI 1:25,000 Mourne Country Outdoor Pursuits Map.
Start & Finish: The circuit starts and finishes at the large parking area for Donard Park at the southern end of Newcastle town (grid reference: J375305). Newcastle is generally reached via the A2 Belfast-Newry road.

INTRODUCTION
At 767m, Slieve Commedagh is the second highest peak in Ulster. Yet it fails to attract a commensurate amount of attention from walkers. Why? Because it also has the perhaps unfortunate pleasure of being

the closest neighbour to Slieve Donard, the highest peak in the province. The 86m height difference between the two summits means that while Slieve Donard is a magnet for even casual walkers, Slieve Commedagh is often overlooked all together.

This is an easily accessible, relatively compact and varied circuit. Firm terrain and straightforward navigation make for generally easy progress, with the slight exception of the descent from Slieve Commedagh summit. Walkers wanting to adapt the route could easily make a more compact circuit of the summit and return via the Glen River Track. For a short walk it is also well worth exploring Donard Wood and the Glen River Track as an outing in its own right.

THE ROUTE

Leave the car park via a tarmac lane in the south-western corner. Within 30m you arrive at a bridge over the Glen River. Do not cross the bridge, but join an earthen path along the right-hand bank of the stream. Skirt an area of open grass and enter the trees of Donard Wood. An information board at the edge of the woodland confirms that you are on the Glen River track.

The next 2km are a delight. The trail passes

through mixed woodland as it climbs gradually alongside the waterfalls, chutes and pools of the Glen River. A series of information posts details the history and natural history of the area.

Around 300m after entering the trees you arrive at a stone bridge; cross this and continue to climb along the opposite bank. A cobblestone path then leads through a copse of rhododendron before bringing you to a second bridge, where the track switches back to the right-hand side of the river.

A third bridge is reached but not crossed – stay on the right-hand bank and continue through the pines to a wooden gate. This gate marks the boundary of the woodland; pass through it and you enter open, mountainous terrain. Just beyond the gate on the left is a conspicuous little beehive building, which was used as an ice-house by the Slieve Donard Hotel in the days before refrigeration.

The col at the top of the Glen River track can now be seen ahead, with the prominent dome of Slieve Commedagh to the west and Slieve Donard to the east. Continue to follow the path along the stream, with smooth granite paving making for rapid progress.

The ground steepens significantly as you near

Route 26

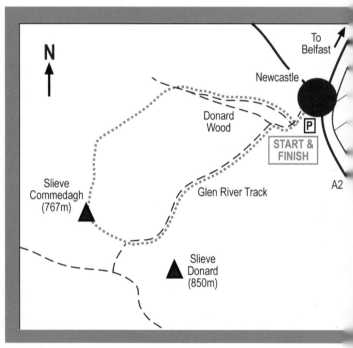

•••••••••• Route Described

the head of the valley and the final climb to the col is short but steady. At the col you are greeted by the Mourne Wall. Turn right just in front of the wall and follow it uphill, with short grass providing easy passage over the steep ground.

The summit plateau of Slieve Commedagh is marked by an angular stone shelter built into the wall, while the cairn marking the summit proper is 150m away to the northeast. At both spots you are rewarded by superb views over the peaks of the northern Mournes, including an unbeatable angle on Slieve Donard.

Descend northwards from the summit cairn. The mountain now narrows to a relatively thin shoulder, and steep cliffs to the east mean care is needed here in poor visibility. Cross the shoulder and continue to descend north over rougher ground.

As you lose height a stone wall becomes visible ahead, running out from the edge of a forestry plantation. Head for the wall, taking care to avoid one or two low cliffs at the base of the slope. Cross the wall and turn right to follow it downhill. A faint path eases your progress over the rough ground, though the final section can still be boggy in wet conditions.

The path joins a gravel track beside a bridge. Turn right, cross the bridge and follow the track into the forest. Keep left at the first junction and right at the second, descending gradually through the plantation. Roughly 1km later veer left at another junction. The woodland now becomes prettier and the banks of the track are swathed with bluebells in the spring.

The end of the track is marked by a sharp left-hand bend. Turn right at the following junction and you will arrive back at the first stone bridge you encountered at the start of the circuit. Turn left onto the footpath just before the bridge and retrace your initial steps downstream to the car park.

ROUTE 27:
COUNTY DOWN — HILL WALK
SLIEVE DONARD

A highly enjoyable circular route over the highest mountain in Northern Ireland. The classic hill walk in the province.

Grade: 4
Time: 4-5 hours
Distance: 9km (5¹/₂ miles)
Ascent: 850m (2800ft)
Maps: OSNI 1:50,000 sheet 29, or OSNI 1:25,000 Mourne Country Outdoor Pursuits Map.
Start & Finish: The walk starts at the Bloody Bridge car park, 3km south of Newcastle on the A2 to Kilkeel (grid reference: J388271). It finishes at the large parking area for Donard Park at the southern end of Newcastle town (grid ref: J375305). Unfortunately these points are separated by 3.5km of road – a road that carries a lot of fast-moving traffic and does not make for pleasant walking. Unless you have two vehicles at your disposal, it is best to leave your car at Donard Park and arrange

alternate transport to the start; consider taking either a local taxi or the No 37 Ulsterbus service.

INTRODUCTION

At 850m, the summit of Slieve Donard is the highest point in Ulster. It is also a supreme viewpoint on a clear day. The mountain towers over the town of Newcastle and its coastal location adds to its charm. Little wonder then that it is a veritable magnet for visiting and local hillwalkers alike.

Many walkers climb Donard from Newcastle, ascending along the Glen River Track and retracing their steps on the descent. This is a rather more interesting, almost-circular variation on that route. It descends via the Glen River but approaches the mountain from the southeast, climbing along the equally lovely Bloody Bridge River. There is sustained and varied interest along the way and with only 3.5km separating the start and finish, there are no great logistical problems involved in reaching the start. Route finding is relatively simple throughout, thanks to a series of maintained footpaths and the guidance of the Mourne Wall.

THE ROUTE

The Bloody Bridge footpath begins just across the road from the southern end of the car park. Pass through a narrow entrance gate and join the well-constructed stone path. The Bloody Bridge River, or the Mid-Pace River as it was once known, rushes over a series of rock slabs beside the path. In early summer the river cuts through a blaze of gorse and is particularly pretty.

Looking back downstream, there's a good view over the original Bloody Bridge. The name itself stems from gruesome events in 1641 when about nine local protestants and their minister were massacred at the bridge.

The path climbs along the right bank, becoming rougher as it progresses. After 1km you may want to cross the river and join a rough quarry track that lies just out of sight up to the left. Alternatively you can continue to pick your way along the river, crossing the stream where necessary. Both options involve 2km of steady ascent before you reach an old quarry.

Leave the quarry via a grassy track on the right and continue to climb to a broad col. Here the view

Route 27

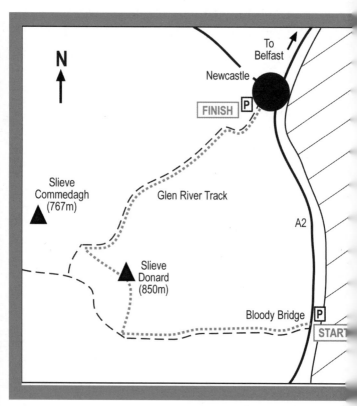

.... Route Described

suddenly opens out westwards across the wider Mournes, with the Annalong Valley immediately beneath you.

The col also marks your rendezvous with the Mourne Wall, which acts as your guide for the next part of the route. Turn right in front of the wall and follow the granite blocks directly up the slopes of Slieve Donard. The ascent is now steep and sustained; some 300m of altitude is gained in less than 1km. Fortunately short grass underfoot makes for fairly easy progress.

Several false summits must be surmounted before the stone tower and trig point of the real summit come into view. The large summit cairn and a smaller one about 100m north have been here in one form or another since early Christian times.

As you would expect, the views from the top are magnificent. On a clear day you can survey the entire Mourne range. To the distant northwest lie Lough Neagh and the Sperrin Mountains, while across the Irish Sea you should be able to identify the Isle of Man and perhaps even parts of the Scottish coast.

The Mourne Wall turns sharply west at the summit. Continue to follow its line and a short, steep descent will bring you to the col beneath Slieve Commedagh.

Here you must leave the wall behind. Turn right onto the path that descends down the centre of the valley to the northeast. The path is partially paved with stone slabs, and while the first section is steep, the gradient soon eases. A stream gathers force beside you as you descend. This is the beginnings of the Glen River which you follow all the way to the end of the route.

Shortly before leaving the mountains you will notice a conspicuous beehive structure on the opposite side of the river. The building was used as an ice house by the Slieve Donard Hotel before the advent of refrigeration. A gate marks the entrance to Donard Wood. Pass through this and you are immediately surrounded by a wonderful mixture of pine and deciduous trees.

The path continues to descend along the Glen River, keeping to the left bank at the first bridge and crossing the river at two subsequent bridges. The woodland and the tumbling falls of the river provide a fitting finale. Finish by passing the grassy expanse of Donard Park to the car park.

ROUTE 28:
COUNTY DOWN – HILL WALK
SLIEVE BEARNAGH & THE SILENT VALLEY

A varied circuit making a back door approach to the distinctive summit of Slieve Bearnagh.

Grade: **4**
Time: **5-6 hours**
Distance: **11km (7 miles)**
Ascent: **850m (2800ft)**
Maps: **OSNI 1:50,000 sheet 29, or OSNI 1:25,000 Mourne Country Outdoor Pursuits Map.**
Start & Finish: The route starts and finishes beneath Ben Crom dam, around 12km north of Kilkeel (grid reference: J314254). The dam is accessed via the Silent Valley Mountain Park; the A2 Newcastle-Kilkeel road has several signs pointing the way. Park at the car park beside the Silent Valley visitor centre.

INTRODUCTION
This route circles high above Ben Crom Reservoir as it explores the mountains at the head of the Silent

Valley. You will need to negotiate some steep ascents and rough terrain as you visit summits such as Slievelamagan (704m) and Slieve Bearnagh (739m). Navigation is helped in parts by footpaths and the Mourne Wall but in other areas you cross open mountain slopes and you will need to rely on your own skills.

As you enter the Silent Valley, the first area you come to is a 200-acre mountain park beneath the Silent Valley Reservoir. The pristine ornamental gardens contrast starkly with the wild backdrop and are a throwback to the Victorian values of 1923, when work on the dam began.

The Mourne granite proved awkward to tame, however, and the dam was eventually completed after ten years of difficulties. The experience deterred the authorities from building another dam in the adjacent Annalong Valley; instead they transferred a considerable flow from the Annalong catchment through a tunnel beneath Slieve Binnian. In the 1950s increased demand prompted the building of the higher Ben Crom dam. Today the Silent and Annalong Valleys provide 130 million litres of water per day, much of it piped underground to Belfast.

It is worth saving the route until the summer months, when a shuttle bus runs between the Silent Valley visitor centre and Ben Crom dam. The bus operates daily in July and August, and on weekends during May, June and September. At all other times of the year you will have to walk. Allow up to two hours extra for the 8km of traffic-free tarmac along the Silent Valley Reservoir. There is a charge for vehicles and pedestrians entering the Silent Valley Mountain Park and the shuttle bus costs an additional £1.20 return.

To extend the circuit, consider adding ascents of Slieve Meelmore, Slieve Meelbeg or Doan.

THE ROUTE

Begin by climbing the steps on the right-hand side of Ben Crom dam. Cross the fence around the reservoir and climb northeast, crossing the steep lower slopes of Slieve Binnian on your way to the boggy col between Binnian and Slievelamagan.

At the col, join a faint footpath leading northeast up the boulder-strewn slopes of Slievelamagan. The ascent is steady with little respite in the gradient. The view from the top is as good as you would expect from the most central

Route 28

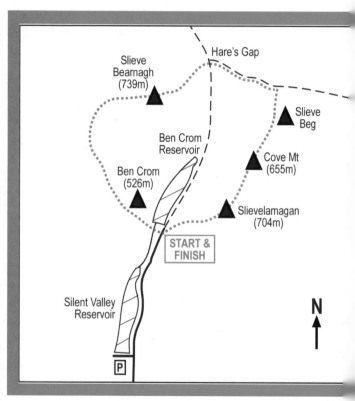

.... Route Described

peak in the Mournes. Especially memorable is the view to the northwest, where Slieve Bearnagh looms over the dark waters of Ben Crom.

Follow the path north from the summit. Descend across a col before climbing slightly across the uninspiring hump of Cove Mountain. Another short descent is followed by a choice of either contouring around the western slopes of Slieve Beg or climbing straight over the top to reach the well-worn path of the Brandy Pad.

Turn left and follow the Brandy Pad west towards the conspicuous green notch of Hare's Gap. About halfway to Hare's Gap the path rounds a small gully and passes behind a curious pillar-like boulder. You are now at the very head of the Silent Valley and there are tremendous views into the deep basin of Ben Crom.

Continue along the Brandy Pad to Hare's Gap, where you meet the Mourne Wall. The Mourne Wall is another water-related construction, built between 1910 and 1922 to encircle the watershed of the Silent and Annalong Valleys.

Turn left in front of the wall and climb south-west up a short flight of steps above Hare's Gap. A short section of flatter ground offers brief respite before the slope steepens again and does not relent until you arrive at Bearnagh's North Tor.

A path skirts the southern side of North Tor and rejoins the Mourne Wall in the col between Bearnagh's twin tops. The name Slieve Bearnagh translates as 'gapped mountain' and probably refers to this feature. A short climb brings you up to the huge Summit Tor. On a good day you will have little trouble appreciating why the combination of granite outcrops and magnificent views make this one of the best-loved peaks in the Mournes.

Follow the south side of the wall as it zigzags on top of Bearnagh, then plunges steeply west to the col between Bearnagh and Slieve Meelmore. At the col join a rough path heading southwest around the base of Slieve Meelmore and Slieve Meelbeg.

Follow the path past Blue Lough on the left, then head south across broken ground towards Ben Crom River. Pick up a faint path beside the river and follow it southeast. When the path peters out, keep contouring across the slopes of Ben Crom to reach a point overlooking a footbridge on the Mill River.

Descend steeply to the bridge, cross the river, and you will arrive back at the road beneath Ben Crom dam.

ROUTE 29:
COUNTY DOWN — HILL WALK
THE BRANDY PAD

A linear route following an old smuggler's trail across the northern Mournes.

Grade: 3
Time: 4-5 hours
Distance: 11km (7 miles)
Ascent: 420m (1380ft)
Maps: OSNI 1:50,000 sheet 29, or OSNI 1:25,000 Mourne Country Outdoor Pursuits Map.
Start & Finish: The route starts at the Trassey Track car park, located around 9km west of Newcastle (grid reference: J312314). From Newcastle town centre, head west towards Bryansford. In Bryansford, turn left along the B180 Hilltown road. Around 4km later, turn left onto a minor road. The Trassey Track car park is situated on the left around 1.5km along this road.

The walk finishes at the Bloody Bridge car park, located 3km south of Newcastle on the A2 to Kilkeel (grid reference: J388271).

INTRODUCTION

The Mournes have one of the best networks of paths of any mountain range in Ireland, many of which were originally created by smugglers and the hooves of their heavily laden ponies.

Smuggling was endemic in the kingdom of Mourne during the eighteenth and ninteenth centuries, aided and abetted by a lonely coast and a mountainous hinterland into which illicit cargos could rapidly disappear. Tobacco, wine, spirits, leather, silk and spices were brought in on manoeuvrable schooners called wherries, and landed on isolated beaches. The goods would then be spirited through the mountains on the path known as the Brandy Pad to be distributed inland. The village of Hilltown was a favourite destination, and by 1835 almost half the houses in the village were pubs. The local public benefited greatly from the trade and their complicity was one reason why smuggling in the region continued for so long.

This route follows the Brandy Pad from the Trassey Track, crossing the head of the Ben Crom and Annalong Valleys before descending to the sea via the Bloody Bridge footpath. The route follows tracks or paths throughout, and navigation is relatively straightforward. It is a good option if the summits are lost in cloud or if you want to cross the wild heart of the Mournes without the exertion of a major ascent.

The path is described in its purest form, as a linear route. If you don't have two vehicles it can be adapted to a near-circuit from Newcastle. From Newcastle head west along the old Ulster Way, which starts at the Shimna River bridge on the town's promenade. Pass through Castle Park, Tipperary Wood and Tollymore Forest to reach the start of the Trassey Track. The route is waymarked throughout and is also indicated on the OS map. From the finish at Bloody Bridge it is relatively simple to take the number 37 Ulsterbus or a local taxi for the 3.5km back to Newcastle. Allow 6-7 hours for this 21km (12¹/₂ miles) variation.

THE ROUTE

From the Trassey Track car park, turn left along the tarmac lane. After 100m turn left again onto a gravel track marked with an information board. Pass over the stile beside the entrance gate and

Route 29

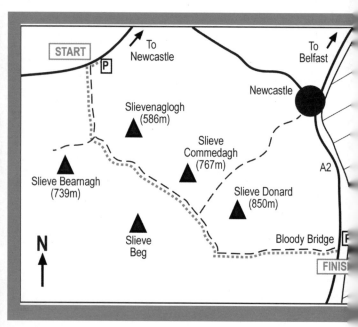

.... Route Described

follow the wide, stony track south along a forestry plantation.

Two more gates with adjacent stiles bring you to the open mountains. Continue to follow the Trassey Track south, winding through a couple of gentle switchbacks before straightening up for the ascent to Hare's Gap. Around 1.5km from the end of the forest you arrive at several track junctions. Keep left at all junctions and cross a couple of streams, now following a much rougher path up the steep, rugged slope to the col itself.

At Hare's Gap you meet the Mourne Wall. Cross the wall and follow the Brandy Pad east across the southern slopes of Slievenaglogh. You are now at the head of the Silent Valley and there are tremendous views south over the enclosed basin that holds the Ben Crom Reservoir.

Pass behind a curious pillar-like boulder, then begin the steady ascent to the col between Slieve Commedagh and Slieve Beg. At a junction just beyond the col, keep left along the main path. You are now at the head of the Annalong Valley. While the Brandy Pad is the most famous smuggling route in the Mournes, it would have been accessed from several different bays along the coast. The

Carrick Little Track at the entrance to Annalong Valley also originated as an off-shoot of this smuggling network.

Contour across steep ground beneath the pinnacles known as The Castles, then swing southeast across the slopes of Slieve Donard, Northern Ireland's highest peak. A final climb brings you back to the Mourne Wall at the col between Donard and Chimney Rock Mountain.

Cross a stile over the wall and begin to descend east towards the sea. The path leads down to an old quarry, where you join a rough vehicle track. Descend along the track for almost 2km to a series of switchbacks. Here you should turn left off the track and descend a short distance north to reach the Bloody Bridge River.

Pick up a rough path that descends along the left bank of the river. The path consolidates as it loses height and the water rushes over a series of rock slabs beside you. The original Bloody Bridge can be seen below, named in memory of a gruesome massacre in 1641 when nine local protestants and their minister were murdered at the bridge.

Pass through a narrow entrance gate at the bottom of the path and cross the road to the car park.

ROUTE 30:
COUNTY DOWN — HILL WALK
ANNALONG VALLEY

A strenuous circuit in the heart of the Mournes that can be adapted to suit the keenest of hillwalkers.

Grade: 5
Time: 7–8 hours
Distance: 17.5 km (11 miles)
Ascent: 1080m (3540ft)
Maps: OSNI 1:50,000 sheet 29, or OSNI 1:25,000 Mourne Country Outdoor Pursuits Map.
Start & Finish: The circuit starts and finishes at Carrick Little car park, around 4km west of Annalong village (grid reference: J345219). Annalong village is situated on the A2, 9km north of Kilkeel and 11km south of Newcastle. In the centre of Annalong, turn northwest opposite a church and head up Majors Hill Road. Roughly 2km later, turn right onto Oldtown Road. Carrick Little car park is situated on the opposite side of a T-Junction some 2km further on.

INTRODUCTION

For many walkers, the Annalong Valley is the very centre of activity in the Mournes. This is hardly surprising, given that the three highest peaks in Northern Ireland (Slieve Donard, Slieve Commedagh and Slieve Binnian) lie around its perimeter. The circumnavigation of the valley is one of the area's classic walks, though the exact route – which summit to visit and which to leave out – can be adapted to personal preference.

The circuit described here takes in Slievelamagan (704m), Cove Mountain (655m), Slieve Beg (590m) and Slieve Donnard (850m). Tracks and informal footpaths are followed for much of the route, and the Mourne wall helps with route finding. Nonetheless, the proximity of several cliffs and the mountainous nature of the terrain make solid navigation skills a necessity. The length and total ascent of the route also mean that it is best suited to more experienced walkers.

Those who want to extend the route should consider including an ascent of Slieve Binnian (747m), the peak that guards the southern end of the valley. You will add a further 2km and 400m of ascent to the day's tally if you choose this option. Alternatively, the route can be shortened by omitting the ascent of Slieve Donard.

THE ROUTE

Begin by heading along the track situated immediately east of Carrick Little car park. The track climbs steadily north, passing several ruined cottages on the left. After approximatelly 1km you arrive at the Mourne Wall, cut here by a gate and a wooden stile.

If you want to add an ascent of Slieve Binnian, turn left and follow the Mourne Wall up steep slopes to the northwest. If you are happy to bypass this peak, continue straight ahead on the Carrick Little Track.

The stone-strewn track skirts the western boundary of Annalong Wood. Keep left at several subsequent junctions, climbing gradually northwest toward the prominent col between Slieve Binnian and Slievelamagan. The track passes to the west of Blue Lough and beneath the overhanging rock face of Buzzard's Roost before reaching the col. Views now open up to the north and west, where the spiked crest of Slieve Bearnagh rises across Ben Crom Reservoir.

Route 30

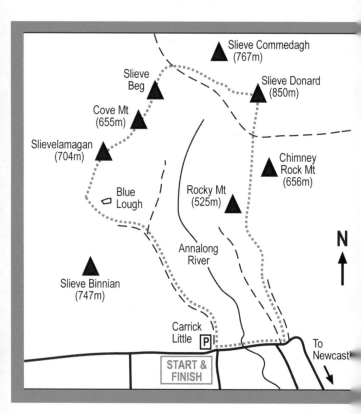

.... Route Described

Turn northeast at the col and begin to climb steeply up the boulder-strewn slopes of Slievelamagan. The ascent is sustained but relatively short-lived. Slievelamagan lies at the centre of an impressive circle of peaks, and the 360° panorama from its summit takes in most of the Kingdom of Mourne.

Descend northeast to the col between Slievelamagan and Cove Mountain. The eastern side of this ridge of peaks is defined by a series of rocky crags, and you climb past the cliffs of Upper Cove on the ascent to Cove Mountain. A descent northwest then leads to another col and over a stream.

The route now veers northeast again and begins to climb towards the summit of Slieve Beg. Near the bottom of the ascent you will pass a dramatic gash in the cliffs that is known as the Devil's Coachroad. From the summit, a short descent northwest brings you to the well-trodden trail known as the Brandy Pad.

Turn right onto the Brandy Pad. You must now decide whether you want to embark on a further 300m climb to the summit of Slieve Donard. If not, keep to right along the main trail and traverse around the southwestern slopes of Donard until you rejoin the Mourne Wall.

If your energy levels permit a visit to the highest point in Ulster, turn left off the Brandy Pad after 600m. Climb to the col between Slieve Commedagh and Slieve Donard, where you meet the Mourne Wall again. Cross the stile and turn right, following the wall up the steep slope to the stone tower at the summit of Slieve Donard. The views now extend over the Irish Sea and County Down coastline.

Turn southwest at the summit and trace the wall steeply downhill. At the base of the descent, a stile marks your return to the Brandy Pad. Cross the wall here and turn left to follow its line south. You must now cross the wet expanse of the Bog of Donard, a task that can involve acrobatic manoeuvres. About 1km later, where the wall makes a slight left turn, climb a few metres to the right and pick up a firmer footpath.

The path passes Rocky Mountain (whose summit can be reached via a slight detour to the west) and then consolidates into a track. Follow the track and descend south to Annalong Wood. Here you come to a junction with the Dunnywater Track; turn left and follow this to the road. Once at the road, turn right and follow the tarmac for 1.5km back to Carrick Little car park.

ROUTE 31:
COUNTY DOWN — HILL WALK
ROSTREVOR FOREST

This short but rewarding circuit offers all the character of a hill walk without too much of the toil.

Grade: 2
Time: 1¹/₂-2 hours
Distance: 3.5km (2 miles)
Ascent: 265m (870ft)
Maps: OSNI 1:50,000 sheet 29, or OSNI 1:25,000 Mourne Country Outdoor Pursuits Map.
Start & Finish: The circuit starts and finishes at the upper parking area on the Rostrevor Forest Drive (grid reference: J195174). To reach the area first travel to Rostrevor, generally accessed via the A2 from Newry. From Rostrevor, continue east along the A2 towards Kilkeel. After 1km turn left at a junction signed for Rostrevor Forest and Kilbroney Park. Once inside the park, follow signs for the Forest Drive to the upper car park. There is plenty of space for vehicles but motorists are warned not to leave valuables on display.

INTRODUCTION

Rostrevor Forest in County Down is something of a gem for recreational walkers. On one hand it has all the advantages of a serviced park; visitor facilities include playing fields, picnic sites, a café and an information office. Yet this is not your average forest reserve. Situated above Carlingford Lough on the southern edge of the Mournes, mountain views rather than tree trunks dominate the route.

The forest has three waymarked walking trails between 2km and 7km long. The highest and most scenic path is described here. The Slieve Martin Trail may be relatively short at 3.5km but it spends most of its time above the trees. The summit of Slieve Martin provides the high point at 485m and views are impressive throughout.

The ascent and descent are steady from start to finish but a maintained path eases your passage as much as possible. The circuit is recommended particularly as an introduction to mountain walking for young children.

THE ROUTE

The Slieve Martin Trail is marked by blue arrows on wooden posts and begins from the information board at the top of the car park.

Start by following the gravel track to the left of the notice board. The track sweeps round to the right and crosses a small stone bridge before beginning a steady ascent around the western slopes of Slieve Meen. After 400m turn left off the main track onto a smaller footpath. You are already above the tree line and there are extensive views over Rostrevor to the northwest.

Continue along the gravel path, climbing more steeply to the top of a spur. The long sea inlet of Carlingford Lough can now be seen below, backed by the rugged profile of the Cooley Mountains.

On the crest of the spur itself lies the Cloghmore Stone. Cloghmore translates literally as great stone. The scientific explanation for the 40-ton granite boulder is that it was deposited here by a glacier during the last Ice Age. Local legend offers a more colourful account, however. According to myth, the rock was hurled to its current position by the Irish giant Finn

Route 31

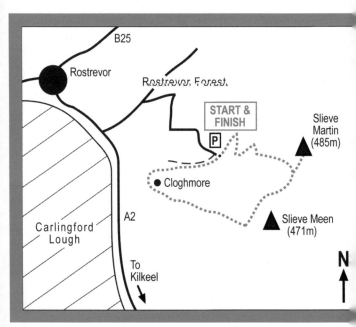

.... Route Described

MacCumhaill during a skirmish with a Scottish counterpart.

The path continues around the back of the boulder and begins to trace a wide arc around the western slopes of Slieve Meen (471m). The angle of ascent eases as you progress and the track turns from gravel to grass underfoot. The summit of Slieve Martin – topped by a concrete trig pillar and nearby radio mast – is clearly visible to the north.

At the northeastern corner of the circuit, the trail rounds a left-hand bend and descends into the forest. If you want to visit the summit of Slieve Martin, bear right along an informal footpath here. The junction is not signed but the summit path leads off along a line of fence posts and is relatively easy to spot.

Follow the fence for around 100m then turn right. A short, steep climb brings you up the final slope to the top. Views from the summit are wide ranging, with Slieve Binnian and Slieve Donard dominating the skyline to the northeast. On a clear day the outlines of the Isle of Man and Howth Peninsula can also be seen across the Irish Sea to the east and south.

Retrace your steps from the summit back to

the main trail and turn right. The path begins to descend immediately, plunging deep into the trees. The darkness and proximity of the towering pines come as quite a contrast after the open spaces of the first part of the route.

Follow the trail through a number of switchbacks, descending rapidly through the trees. Keep left at a final signed junction and you will soon arrive back at the car park.

ROUTE 32:
COUNTY DOWN — HILL WALK
ROCKY RIVER CIRCUIT

A rugged circumnavigation of the Rocky River valley in the lesser-known eastern Mournes.

Grade: **4**
Time: **5-6 hours**
Distance: **12km (7^1/$_2$ miles)**
Ascent: **875m (2870ft)**
Maps: **OSNI 1:50,000 sheet 29, or OSNI 1:25,000 Mourne Country Outdoor Pursuits Map.**
Start & Finish: **The circuit starts and finishes at a car park beside Rocky River Bridge (Grid Reference: J233277). The closest settlement to the area is Hilltown. From there, take the B27 east towards Kilkeel and turn right after 3km. The car park is located 1.5km later, on the western side of the road just before the bridge. There is space for around fifteen vehicles and an adjacent picnic area.**

INTRODUCTION
This circuit visits the five peaks around the Rocky

River valley: Rocky Mountain (405m), Slievemoughanmore (559m), Pigeon Rock Mountain (534m), Cock Mountain (505m) and Hen Mountain (354m). Each mountain has its own distinct character but some rough ground must be negotiated between the summits.

The route allows a bird's eye view of Spelga Reservoir, which supplies water to Portadown and Banbridge. Before the construction of the dam in 1957 the area was a large mountain pasture known as the 'Deer's Meadow'. Local people would drive their cattle here at the start of the summer and live beside their animals throughout the grazing season. The practice was known as booleying, and the remains of several seasonal huts or booleys have been found around the reservoir.

Navigational skills are required for this route when weather is bad, though Batt's Wall provides guidance over southern sections. For tired walkers there is a handy escape option halfway round. To avoid the final three peaks of the circuit, turn northwest towards the Rocky River Track at the col between Slievemoughanmore and Pigeon Rock Mountain. To extend the walk, continue south from Tornamrock and include ascents of

Shanlieve (626m) and Eagle Mountain (638m).

THE ROUTE

Cross the road from the car park and follow a farm track past the left of a house. After 600m a metal gate provides access to the open mountains. Follow the track for a further 500m and then turn southwest towards Rocky Mountain.

You will need to cross Rocky River at the base of the mountain; a relatively straightforward boulder hop unless water levels are high. A steady climb then leads up grass and heather slopes to the low cairn that marks the summit. Good views stretch south from here down the Kilbroney Valley to Carlingford Lough.

Turn southeast and descend across a col before climbing again to Tornamrock. Pass to the right of a rock tor and continue south along the long, heathery plateau before descending gently southeast towards Rocky Water.

Your next destination is Windy Gap, the col on the skyline to the southwest. A stream leads up the centre of the valley towards the gap but the ground is rough along its banks. Easier terrain can be found by climbing a short distance west and

Route 32

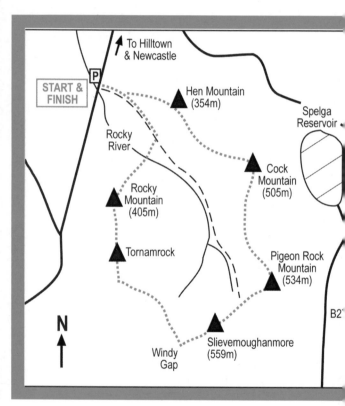

·········· Route Described

joining the broken footpath of the old Ulster Way.

Windy Gap is dissected by Batt's Wall, an off-shoot of the main Mourne Wall. Use two large wooden stiles to cross the wall and then head northeast up the slopes of Slievemoughanmore. Keep the wall on your left and follow a path up the steep ground, with good views of Eagle Mountain behind you.

When the gradient eases towards the top of the mountain, look for a place where the stones have collapsed and cross to the north side of the wall. The summit cairn that marks the highest point of the route is a short distance away, providing great views over both the Rocky River valley and the rest of the Mourne range to the northeast.

Return to the wall and descend steeply to the col beneath Pigeon Rock Mountain. If you want to avoid any more climbing you could turn left here and follow the path down to the Rocky River Track. To complete the full circuit, continue straight ahead, still tracing the northern side of Batt's Wall.

The ascent to Pigeon Rock Mountain is much more gradual. Shortly before the summit, turn left alongside the wall and cross the edge of a shallow pool. The small summit cairn is located at the point where the wall turns east once more. Spelga Reservoir can now be seen below you to the northeast.

Leave the wall at the summit of Pigeon and continue northwest, descending grassy slopes to a wide, meadow-like col. Keep to the left side of the col to avoid wet ground in the centre. Now comes the last big climb of the route. Head directly up the heather-cloaked slopes of Cock Mountain, aiming to pass directly between the twin peaks on the summit.

From the top of Cock Mountain it is a surprise to see the tors of Hen Mountain below you. Descend steeply and cross the shallow col towards Hen. The granite outcrops are popular with rock climbers and it is well worth detouring around them to explore them in more detail.

When you are ready, head for the base of the westernmost tor. A path descends from here to the metal gate at the bottom of the Rocky River Track. Simply follow the track back to the car park.

ROUTE 33:
COUNTY DOWN — HILL WALK
EAGLE MOUNTAIN

Good tracks and paths allow for a relatively easy exploration of this Mourne summit.

Grade: 3
Time: 3-4 hours
Distance: 8km (5 miles)
Ascent: 490m (1610 ft)
Maps: OSNI 1:50,000 sheet 29, or OSNI 1:25,000 Mourne Country Outdoor Pursuits Map.
Start & Finish: The route starts and finishes at the end of a minor road around 8km northwest of Kilkeel (grid reference: J263206). From Kilkeel, take the B27 north for 5km and turn left towards Attical village. Turn left in the centre of Attical and continue southwest for a further kilometre. Watch out for a Gaelic football pitch on the right. Turn right immediately before the pitch onto a lane signed 'Sandy Brae'. Follow the lane past a water treatment plant and continue for another kilometre, where the road ends at a ford. Park in a

clearing on the left opposite several large sheds.

INTRODUCTION

Eagle Mountain (638m) is the highest summit of the western Mournes. A steep-sided peak whose southeastern flanks fall away in a line of sheer cliffs, Eagle boasts some of the highest crags in the Mournes as well as some of the best views. Slightly removed from the compact knot of peaks that make up the core of the range, Eagle and its neighbouring 'outliers' are significantly less frequented than the more famous summits to the east.

The route described here is relatively straightforward, approaching Eagle Mountain from the south. Much of the route follows well-defined tracks and footpaths, though the descent involves some cliff-top walking and passes over rougher terrain. Batt's Wall offers a reassuring navigational aid, though care is needed in the vicinity of the cliffs in poor visibility. The circuit can easily be expanded by adding side trips to the summits of Slievemoughanmore and/or Shanlieve.

THE ROUTE

From the ford, begin by crossing the concrete

footbridge over the river. The public road ends at the ford and the track that continues to Windy Gap crosses private ground, necessitating a small, signed detour to the west. Turn immediately left on the northern bank of the river and follow a narrow path west along the southern boundary of a house. After 50m you come to a stile; cross this and follow the path north and then northeast, taking care to avoid several patches of wet ground.

The path rejoins the Windy Gap track on the banks of the Pigeon Rock River. Turn left and begin to climb gently along the track and before long you will arrive at a fork. A rougher track continues ahead, heading north towards Slievemoughanmore. This is the route to take if you want to add the ascent of Slievemoughanmore to the circuit. To continue directly towards Eagle Mountain, keep left along the main track.

The gradient now increases and you climb steadily beneath the imposing buttresses and gullies that girdle the eastern side of Eagle Mountain. As the cliffs give way to steep rock slabs you will notice a partially quarried area on the left, where the natural angular bedding of the rock aided the extraction of huge blocks of granite. During the

Route 33

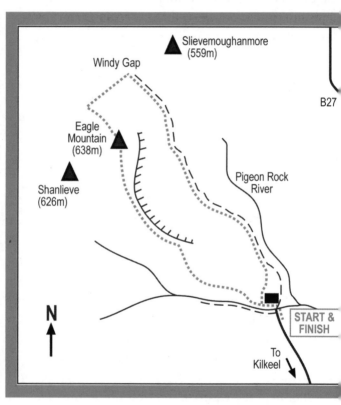

·········· Route Described

1800s and early 1900s in particular, large quantities of granite were exported from this area to face prominent buildings in Britain.

The track ends beneath the quarry but an informal path continues northwest, arriving at Batt's Wall a short distance above Windy Gap. Batt's Wall is a miniature imitation of the Mourne Wall, built to enclose the Batt's Estate. For modern walkers it provides a useful navigational tool.

Turn left and climb steeply beside the wall, following a well-worn path. The views now really begin to open out, with the granite tors of Hen Mountain particularly prominent to the north. As you near the top of the mountain the wall turns sharply southeast. Turn left alongside the wall, now climbing more gently. In a few hundred metres the wall swings back to the southwest. Fifty metres beyond the apex of this second turn a small cairn marks the summit of Eagle Mountain.

The views over the high Mournes are now at their best. To the northeast the tors of Slieve Bearnagh and the summit slopes of Slieve Donard can be seen beyond the intervening whaleback of Slieve Muck. To the east Slieve Binnian displays the superb rock castles on its crest. To the north and west the panorama extends to the distant profiles of the Sperrins and Belfast Hills.

If you want to visit Shanlieve, half a kilometre further along Batt's Wall to the southeast, it is best to make an out-and-back trip from the summit of Eagle Mountain.

When you are ready to descend, head south from Eagle Mountain. Cross heather-clad slopes to the top of the cliffs and follow a narrow path southeast along the cliff edge. The path becomes indistinct as you descend, and at times it is little more than a rough sheep track through the heather.

Head towards the house that you walked around at the very beginning of the route. Re-cross the stile at the southern edge of the house boundary and return across the footbridge to the parking area.

ROUTE 34:
COUNTY DOWN – HILL WALK
THE BINNIANS

An excellent circuit over two distinctive summits, offering some sustained high-level walking.

Grade: 4
Time: 4½-5½ hours
Distance: 13km (8 miles)
Ascent: 625m (1900ft)
Maps: OSNI 1:50,000 sheet 29, or OSNI 1:25,000 Mourne Country Outdoor Pursuits Map.
Start & Finish: The route starts and finishes at Carrick Little car park, roughly 4km west of Annalong village (grid reference: J345219). Annalong village is situated on the A2, 9km north of Kilkeel and 11km south of Newcastle. In the centre of Annalong, turn northwest opposite a church and begin up Majors Hill Road. Around 2km later, turn right onto Oldtown Road. Carrick Little car park is situated on the opposite side of a T-junction some 2km later.

Introduction

At the southerneastern corner of the Mourne Mountains two summits stand together like big brother and little brother. Thanks to their location, Slieve Binnian (747m) and Wee Binnian (459m) provide fantastic views over both the rugged heartland of the Mournes and the pastoral coast-line to the south.

The most distinctive feature of these moun-tains is not their views though, but the granite tors that crown their summits. Slieve Binnian, in par-ticular has several clusters of tors scattered across its broad ridge, making it one of the most interest-ing summits in Ireland. The tors are a feature of the glacial past, other local examples being found at the top of Slieve Bearnagh and Hen Mountain. It is thought these summits were left above the ice sheets as nunatacks during the last ice age. Exposure to severe frost weathering meant that soil and weaker layers of granite were eroded away to leave these fascinating formations.

Although Binnian appears as a steep pyramid from the south, in reality it's a much more extensive mountain. This route offers a trip along its entire length, with almost 2km of walking above 600m. Though it is a fairly short circuit by some standards, the steep ascent makes it feel quite strenuous.

Informal paths have formed over much of the route but you will still need good navigation skills in bad weather. The route begins with 2.5km of road walking. If you have two vehicles this tarmac section can be avoided by leaving a second car near Brackenagh Cross Water Bridge, 2.5km west of the start.

THE ROUTE

From Carrick Little car park, join the road and walk west along the tarmac for 2.5km to Brackenagh Cross Water Bridge. Cross the bridge and, 50m later, look for a track that leads north off the road. Turn right and head up the track, climbing steadily towards the col between Moolieve and Wee Binnian. After 500m the track breaks up into several rougher trails. Keep straight on, still heading directly towards the col.

Just beneath the col you reach the Mourne Wall and a heavy iron gate. At this point you have a choice of routes. For the adventurous option, stay on the southern side of the wall and follow it

Route 34

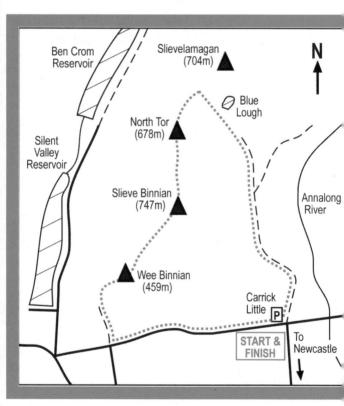

.... Route Described

northwest. As you round the side of the mountain you come to a deep gully that cuts the main tor in two. Climb through the gully, making a strenuous heave over a rock step halfway up. Several rock climbs start from this gully and the scramble up the gully itself was given a climbing grade in the Victorian era.

For the easier option, go through the gate and follow the northern side of the wall towards Wee Binnian. Where the wall ends at the foot of the summit tor, follow a path around the northern slopes of the mountain.

Whichever way you reach Wee Binnian, you must now descend northeast to a col. The shoulder of Slieve Binnian now rises ahead of you in a single, relentless sweep of more than 300m. The Mourne Wall runs directly up the shoulder and you should climb steeply along the southern side of this. Extensive views open up to the south as you gain height and compensate for the exertion.

The wall peters out a short distance beneath the summit at the foot of some steep rock slabs. Climb to the right of the slabs and head up into a gap between two subsidiary tors. Exit the gap at the eastern side of the mountain and join a well-defined path around the base of the summit tor.

From the summit the path heads north across a broad shoulder, descending gently towards several smaller tors on the otherwise flat terrain. These are known as the Black Castles, and the path skirts across the rocky base of the largest outcrop. The view across the Mournes is superb from here, encompassing virtually every peak in the range.

Beyond the Black Castles the path descends to a broad col. The North Tor is now 400m away to the northeast and the path suggests that most people skip point 678m and contour directly to this tor.

Head around the western side of North Tor and begin the main descent. Keep to the shoulder of Binnian's north ridge, which becomes narrower as you near the col beneath Slievelamagan.

Once in the col, join a path that descends southeast past Blue Lough. The path becomes a track above Annalong Wood, then turns into a laneway. Continue straight ahead at all junctions to arrive back at Carrick Little car park.